D0281767

endorsed for
BTEC

REVISE BTEC NATIONAL
Information Technology

REVISION GUIDE

Series Consultant: Harry Smith

Authors: Alan Jarvis and Daniel Richardson

A note from the publisher

In order to ensure that this resource offers high-quality support for the associated Pearson qualification, it has been through a review process by the awarding body. This process confirms that this resource fully covers the teaching and learning content of the specification or part of a specification at which it is aimed. It also confirms that it demonstrates an appropriate balance between the development of subject skills, knowledge and understanding, in addition to preparation for assessment.

Endorsement does not cover any guidance on assessment activities or processes (e.g. practice questions or advice on how to answer assessment questions) included in the resource nor does it prescribe any particular approach to the teaching or delivery of a related course.

While the publishers have made every attempt to ensure that advice on the qualification and its assessment is accurate, the official specification and associated assessment guidance materials are the only authoritative source of information and should always be referred to for definitive guidance.

Pearson examiners have not contributed to any sections in this resource relevant to examination papers for which they had prior responsibility.

Examiners will not use endorsed resources as a source of material for any assessment set by Pearson.

Endorsement of a resource does not mean that the resource is required to achieve this Pearson qualification, nor does it mean that it is the only suitable material available to support the qualification, and any resource lists produced by the awarding body shall include this and other appropriate resources.

For the full range of Pearson revision titles across KS2, KS3, GCSE, Functional Skills, AS/A Level and BTEC visit:
www.pearsonschools.co.uk/revise

Published by Pearson Education Limited, 80 Strand, London, WC2R 0RL.

www.pearsonschoolsandfecolleges.co.uk

Copies of official specifications for all Edexcel qualifications may be found on the website: www.edexcel.com

Text and illustrations © Pearson Education Limited 2017
Typeset and illustrated by Kamae Design
Produced by Out of House Publishing
Cover illustration by Miriam Sturdee

The right of Alan Jarvis and Daniel Richardson to be identified as authors of this work have been asserted by them in accordance with the Copyright, Designs and Patents Act 1988.

First published 2017

20 19 18 17
10 9 8 7 6 5 4 3 2 1

British Library Cataloguing in Publication Data
A catalogue record for this book is available from the British Library

ISBN 978 1 292 15036 9

Printed in the UK by Bell & Bain

Acknowledgements
The author and publisher would like to thank the following individuals and organisations for permission to reproduce photographs:

(Key: b-bottom; c-centre; l-left; r-right; t-top)

123RF.com: alexlmx 7, Peter Bernik 14t, Innovatedcaptures 13, Olekcii Mach 2t; **Alamy Images:** Sergio Azenha 3t, Cultura Creative 25t, 47t, Ian Dagnall 5l, David Tipling Photo Library 29, Pylyp Fomin 11, Igor Stevanovic 35 (a), Steven May 66, MBI 3b, Phanie 34, Redsnapper 75, Andrzej Tokarski 5r, Uber Images 30; **Fotolia.com:** alexlmx 6tr, Family Business 33t, FreedomMan 22b, Georgejmclittle 33, Monkey Business 47b; **Getty Images:** Future Publishing 1b, Jonathan Kantor 2b; **Press Association Images:** 26; **Rex Shutterstock:** Olly Curtis / Future Publishing 1; **Shutterstock. com:** Africa Studio. 54, Amble Design 28t, Elena Elisseeva 27, ESB Professional 35 (b), Kastianz 11tl, Marco Mayer 57, Morgan Lane Photography 58, Pressmaster 59, Rawpixel.com 4b, vlad.georgescu 37, Vladru 1c

All other images © Pearson Education

We are grateful to the following for permission to reproduce copyright material:

Screenshots:
Microsoft product screenshot(s) reprinted with permission from Microsoft Corporation on pages 9–10, 29, 33, 58–59, pages 66–76, page 90, pages 98–101, pages 103–104.

A note from the publisher
In order to ensure that this resource offers high-quality support for the associated Pearson qualification, it has been through a review process by the awarding body. This process confirms that this resource fully covers the teaching and learning content of the specification or part of a specification at which it is aimed. It also confirms that it demonstrates an appropriate balance between the development of subject skills, knowledge and understanding, in addition to preparation for assessment.

Endorsement does not cover any guidance on assessment activities or processes (e.g. practice questions or advice on how to answer assessment questions), included in the resource nor does it prescribe any particular approach to the teaching or delivery of a related course.

While the publishers have made every attempt to ensure that advice on the qualification and its assessment is accurate, the official specification and associated assessment guidance materials are the only authoritative source of information and should always be referred to for definitive guidance.

Pearson examiners have not contributed to any sections in this resource relevant to examination papers for which they have responsibility.

Examiners will not use endorsed resources as a source of material for any assessment set by Pearson.

Endorsement of a resource does not mean that the resource is required to achieve this Pearson qualification, nor does it mean that it is the only suitable material available to support the qualification, and any resource lists produced by the awarding body shall include this and other appropriate resources.

Introduction

Which units should you revise?

This Revision Guide has been designed to support you in preparing for the externally assessed units of your course. Remember that you won't necessarily be studying all the units included here – it will depend on the qualification you are taking.

BTEC National Qualification	Externally assessed units
Certificate	2 Creating Systems to Manage Information
Extended Certificate and Foundation Diploma	1 Information Technology Systems 2 Creating Systems to Manage Information

Your Revision Guide

Each unit in this Revision Guide contains two types of pages, shown below.

Content pages help you revise the essential content you need to know for each unit.

Skills pages help you prepare for your exam or assessed task. Skills pages have a coloured edge and are shaded in the table of contents.

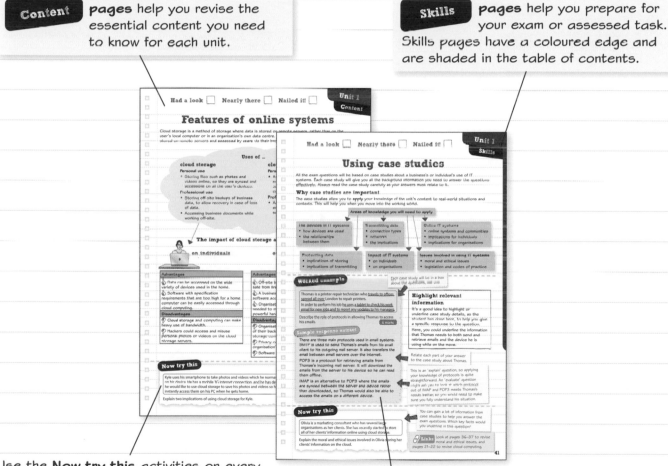

Use the **Now try this** activities on every page to help you test your knowledge and practise the relevant skills.

Look out for the **sample response extracts** to exam questions or set tasks on the skills pages. Post-its will explain their strengths and weaknesses.

Contents

Workbook also available for externally assessed units ISBN 9781292150352

A small bit of small print

Pearson publishes Sample Assessment Material and the Specification on its website. This is the official content and this book should be used in conjunction with it. The questions in Now try this have been written to help you test your knowledge and skills. Remember: the real assessment may not look like this.

Digital devices 1

A digital device is an electronic device that uses digital data (such as 1s and 0s) as opposed to analogue data (such as a sound wave). Here are five commonly used types of device that you need to know about.

① Multifunctional devices

These devices can perform multiple functions, such as inputting and outputting data.

An example is a **touch screen**, which outputs an image while allowing the user to input data by pressing the screen or a multi-functional printer.

② Personal computers

These are small and inexpensive computers for use by individual users.

Examples are **desktops** and **laptops**, which are more portable and have a built-in battery, screen and keyboard.

Force feedback game controllers are multifunctional devices – they can input data and output vibration.

③ Mobile devices

Smartphones and **tablets** are made with portability in mind to give people computer and internet access while on the go.

④ Servers

These powerful computers provide services to other computers connected to a network.

An example is a **mail server** that provides access to email services for all the users on a network.

Web servers store web pages and online content, and serve data to users over the internet.

🔗 **Links** For more on networks, see page 17.

⑤ Entertainment systems

These are devices for watching TV/films (such as **satellite** or **cable digiboxes**), listening to music and playing video games.

Games consoles are entertainment systems with powerful graphics processors that allow users to play video games.

Now try this

Nadeem wants to access the internet while he is travelling to college by train.

(a) Give a type of digital device that would be appropriate for Nadeem to use.

(b) Explain two reasons why the device you chose is appropriate for Nadeem's requirements.

Concentrate on Nadeem's requirements, and the features he most needs when using a device while out of the house, on a train.

Digital devices 2

Digital devices are often developed to make everyday tasks easier, quicker or more cost-effective and to provide efficient, improved access to data. There are four types of digital device that you need to know about.

① Digital cameras

These capture images and videos digitally using an image sensor and store them as digital data on media such as a memory card or hard drive.

Examples are **still** and **video** cameras.

 Links There is more about data storage on page 6.

② Navigation systems

These devices use a GPS (Global Positioning Satellite) receiver to locate the user's position on a digital map and provide directions to a given destination.

An example is an **in-car satnav** which uses GPS location data with software to provide directions to a given destination when driving.

③ Communication devices and systems

These devices can send and receive analogue or digital data to and from another device.

Traditional analogue examples include phones and faxes.

A modern digital example is a **router** which directs data across a network.

WiFi dongles are communication devices that allow your PC to communicate with a router wirelessly.

④ Data capture and collection systems

These devices collect and input data through automated systems rather than direct data entry.

Examples include:

- a **barcode scanner**, which inputs (or reads) a barcode and converts the information into data
- an **optical mark reader**, which reads pencil or pen marks on specially designed printed forms, such as lottery tickets
- an **EPOS** (electronic point of sale) system, which records sales and updates stock levels.

An **RFID reader** reads data stored on a smartcard by being in close proximity to the card. These are often used by payment cards or for stock control.

Now try this

J P Lucy is a chain of small department stores, with five branches.

State two different data capture and collection systems that might be used in the department stores.

Questions with the command word 'identify' don't require long answers. You can give your answer using single words or short sentences.

Uses of digital devices

Digital devices play an increasingly important role in many different areas of our lives. They enhance our social lives and make our work role more efficient. However, sometimes they also have the opposite effect.

Uses of digital devices

Here are some examples of how digital devices are used in six key areas of our lives.

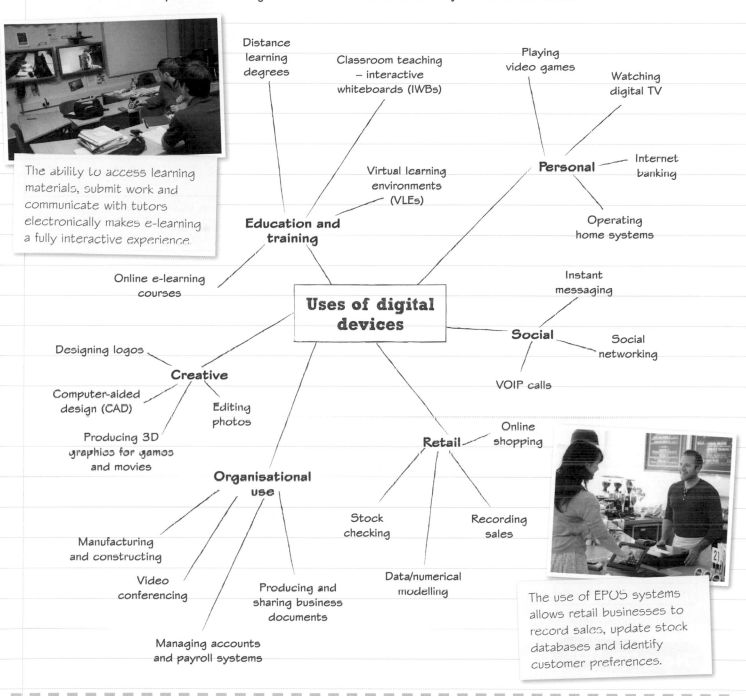

The ability to access learning materials, submit work and communicate with tutors electronically makes e-learning a fully interactive experience.

Distance learning degrees

Classroom teaching – interactive whiteboards (IWBs)

Playing video games

Watching digital TV

Virtual learning environments (VLEs)

Personal

Internet banking

Operating home systems

Education and training

Online e-learning courses

Instant messaging

Uses of digital devices

Social

Social networking

Designing logos

VOIP calls

Creative

Computer-aided design (CAD)

Editing photos

Online shopping

Producing 3D graphics for games and movies

Retail

Organisational use

Stock checking

Recording sales

Manufacturing and constructing

Video conferencing

Producing and sharing business documents

Data/numerical modelling

Managing accounts and payroll systems

The use of EPOS systems allows retail businesses to record sales, update stock databases and identify customer preferences.

Now try this

J P Lucy is a chain of small department stores, with five branches.

Explain how your choice of data capture and collection systems you have identified might be used in the stores and why they would be beneficial to the business.

This is the second part of the question you answered on the previous page. When explaining how J P Lucy might use the data capture and collection systems you identified, focus on the advantages of these systems. How do they help the business?

Input and output devices

Peripheral devices are hardware devices that are not essential to the running of a computer system, but that connect to the system and provide additional functions. The most common types are input and output devices.

🔗 **Links** For more on accessibility devices, see page 5.

Input devices

Device	Features	Example uses
Keyboard	Made up of keys used to input alphanumeric characters and symbols.	• Writing a report • Inputting into a database
Mouse	A pointing device used to select items on screen.	• Navigating a user interface, e.g. by clicking on icons
Scanner	Converts hard copy text or images into a digital format.	• Inputting a photo for editing in graphics software
Graphics tablet	Controls the computer by using a stylus on a tablet.	• Creating digital illustrations
Microphone	Converts analogue signals (sound waves) into electrical signals to be sent to the sound card which converts analogue to digital.	• Talking on VOIP software • Voice recording
Webcam	Inputs video and still images directly into a computer.	• Video conferencing
Sensor	Takes and inputs readings from the physical environment, such as changes in temperature.	• Automated central heating systems • Security systems

Output devices

Device	Features	Example uses
Monitor	Outputs an image to the user, e.g. of the user interface, a photo or a document.	• Viewing the user interface • Watching movies
Projector	Outputs an image onto a wall or screen	
Printer	Produces hard copies of digital documents and images on paper.	• A hard copy of a report • Printing digital photos
Plotter	This specialist type of printer draws to a very high quality on very large paper.	• Drawing vector graphics
Speakers	Amplify analogue signals (sound waves) sent from the sound card for the user to hear.	• Listening to music • Listening to someone during a VOIP call
Headphones	A portable alternative to speakers.	

Now try this

Marit is a graphic designer who produces posters and leaflets. She creates a lot of the digital illustrations for these herself.

State two input devices and two output devices, explaining how they would be useful to Marit in her graphic design work.

The question asks you to 'explain' your choice of input and output devices, so as well as naming the devices, you need to give reasons why they are useful to Marit.

Devices for accessibility and data processing

Peripheral devices have been designed to perform many specialist functions. Two important types are devices that aid accessibility to computer systems, and those that automate data processing for organisations.

Accessibility devices

Some peripheral devices are specifically created to allow accessibility for people with disabilities. For example:

- **trackball** – an easier-to-use alternative to a mouse, consisting of a moveable ball on a base

- **touch screen** or **large key keyboard** – useful for people unable to use a keyboard easily

- **eye motion sensors** and **head motion trackers** – used by people with significantly limited mobility

- **Braille embosser** – a type of printer that outputs text as Braille cells (characters).

Adaptive technologies

These are technologies that have been designed specifically to aid people with disabilities. They include both hardware and software.

Peripheral devices such as a trackerball or eye motion sensors are **hardware** – they are physical items that you can touch.

There are also many types of **software** available to aid accessibility, such as voice recognition software for input and screen reading software for output.

Manual and automatic data processing

There are peripheral devices which can automate the input and processing of data and avoid human errors such as typos during data entry. Some types of data collection, input and processing are more commonly done manually. Here are some examples of both.

Manual processes

- Keying client or product details into a database.
- Entering customers' meal choices into a restaurant's system.
- Marking exam scripts.
- Entering survey responses from a form.

Automatic processes/devices

- **Biometric readers** read fingerprints, hand prints or irises for use in personnel identification systems.
- **Barcode readers** read lines of different thickness and convert them into a string of values. 2D readers read more complex QR-style codes.
- **Optical mark recognition (OMR) readers** automatically read a form and input the data.
- **Radio-frequency identification (RFID) devices** are used in stock taking and race timing systems.
- **Smart meters** accurately record electricity and gas usage and send readings to the energy supplier.

Now try this

Marcus has recently become visually impaired following an accident.

Give two peripheral devices that will allow Marcus to continue using his IT systems.

The question is specifically asking you to identify peripheral devices rather than software. But the peripheral devices you suggest may allow Marcus to use adaptive software.

Storage devices

Storage devices are a type of peripheral device used for storing, backing up and sharing data, usually for individual use where a network is not available.

Hard disk drives ...

are magnetic storage devices, commonly used as the primary internal storage device but can be external.

Characteristics and limitations

👍 Large storage capacity (1 terabyte or more).

👍 Low cost on a per byte basis.

👍 Very reliable.

👎 Slower than SSDs at loading data.

👎 External HDDs are not as portable as some other options.

Solid state drives ...

are flash memory devices commonly used as the primary storage in portable computing devices like tablets and laptops.

Characteristics and limitations

👍 Very fast data read/write speeds.

👍 Low power consumption.

👍 Extremely reliable as they have no moving parts which can be damaged.

👎 Higher cost than HDDs on a per byte basis.

👎 Usually have a lower storage capacity.

👎 Only have a finite number of writes.

SD cards ...

are small flash memory cards that are commonly used for storage in digital cameras and some smartphones.

Characteristics and limitations

👍 Very small and portable.

👍 Easy to transfer between devices with SD card readers.

👎 Very small storage capacity, generally around 64gb – greater capacity is costly.

👎 Various 'enhancements' to the standards, resulting in potential compatibility problems, for example SDHC and SDXC.

USB memory sticks ...

are small flash memory devices that connect through a USB port.

Characteristics and limitations

👍 Extremely portable device.

👍 Compatible with most computer systems via USB ports.

👎 Storage capacity is low when compared to SSDs and HDDs.

👎 Only have a finite number of writes before they break.

👎 Because they are small, they can be lost easily.

Optical disks ...

such as CDs, DVDs and Blu-ray disks are used for software, music and movies.

Characteristics and limitations

👍 Small and portable.

👍 A lot of devices have built in capability to read optical discs, with external devices being inexpensive if needed.

👎 Archival stability of writable media can be questionable.

👎 Fragile and easy to damage.

Magnetic tape ...

is used for large data backups.

Characteristics and limitations

👍 Very large storage capacity.

👍 Very cheap on a per byte basis.

👎 Data is accessed serially which is very slow.

👎 Requires specialist equipment for recording and reading data.

Now try this

Explain two limitations of using a USB memory stick for transferring video footage and graphics between home and office.

Try to explain each limitation you identify in as much detail as possible.

Types of operating system

The operating system is what co-ordinates all the operations of your computer. It manages all the resources on the computer, such as the CPU and RAM, and controls the software and hardware. Without it, your PC would be useless.

Real-time operating systems (RTOS)

Inputs are processed and responded to instantaneously.

Why choose real-time?

- It provides fast response.
- It is best used where inputs must be processed and responded to immediately, such as traffic light and air traffic control systems.

Automatic braking systems (ABS) are an example of a RTOS. The system continuously processes input data to detect obstacles and apply the brakes to avoid collision as required.

Single-user single task operating systems

One user can use the system at a time, and one application can run at a time.

Why choose single-user single task?

- It requires fewer resources.
- It is best used on devices that have limited processing and memory, which could not handle running multiple applications, for example basic mobile phones or a simple handheld game (such as a Virtual Pet).

Single-user multi-tasking operating systems

One user can use the system at a time, but many applications can run simultaneously.

Why choose single-user multi-tasking?

- It allows the user to use several applications at once.
- It is best used on systems where a user needs to be able to switch quickly between applications, for example an office worker using a laptop or desktop PC.

Multi-user operating systems

Many users can use the system at the same time and can run many applications simultaneously.

Why choose multi-user?

- Processing and resources can be shared by multiple-users.
- It is best used where many users need access to the same processing or resources at the same time, for example web servers.

Operating system performance factors

Operating systems require careful maintenance to keep them performing efficiently.

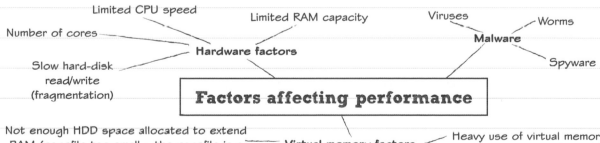

Limited CPU speed

Number of cores

Limited RAM capacity

Viruses ── Worms

Malware

Spyware

Hardware factors

Slow hard-disk read/write (fragmentation)

Factors affecting performance

Not enough HDD space allocated to extend RAM (pagefile too small – the pagefile is a section of the hard disk that is reserved as an extension of the RAM)

Virtual memory factors

Heavy use of virtual memory relies on slow disc transfers rather than the very fast working memory (RAM) data transfers

Now try this

Analyse the factors that affect the performance of an operating system.

You need to demonstrate your ability to use technical vocabulary. You should also cover a range of issues and not just one or two.

The role of the operating system

The operating system on a digital device is the link between the hardware and the software. It passes messages back and forth and carries out instructions from the software to the hardware.

Networking

Operating systems simplify networking in a computer. The operating system implements a number of networking technologies such as:

- the **TCP/IP stack**
- network utility programs like traceroute
- device drivers for the network interface card.

The TCP/IP stack is the set of protocols used for transmitting data over the internet. The data transmission takes place in layers (or steps). The diagram shows how the TCP/IP stack links to the OSI model, which is the standard model used to explain how computers network.

 Links For more on traceroute, see page 10.

 Links For more on protocols, see page 19.

OSI model		TCP/IP
7	Application	Application
6	Presentation	
5	Session	
4	Transport	← TCP →	Transport
3	Network	← IP →	Internet
2	Data link	Network interface
1	Physical	

OSI model   **TCP/IP**

Security

A number of features are commonly built into operating systems to help improve security. These include:

- user authentication
- anti-virus and firewall software
- backup facilities.

Memory management

The operating system manages the computer's resources, such as its memory.

To do this, the operating system decides and tracks:

- which processes to allocate memory to
- how much memory to allocate to each process
- when to un-allocate memory
- transferring data to the pagefile (or swapfile) on the HDD temporarily to free RAM (paging or swapping).

Multi-tasking

Most operating systems allow you to run more than one application simultaneously. To do this, the operating system must be able to allocate resources (CPU, memory, disk space) to each application in order to allow it to complete two or more tasks simultaneously.

Device drivers

An operating system comes with generic device drivers that work with a wide variety of different peripheral devices, allowing them to communicate with your computer. However, most hardware comes supplied with specific drivers to take full advantage of the hardware's capabilities.

Now try this

Describe the ways in which operating systems help to manage memory on an IT system.

 Try to answer the question without looking at the information on this page. Then read the page again to check your answer.

User interfaces

The user interface is a core part of any operating system. It allows the user to interact with the computer system and is the part of the software that has a huge impact on a user in terms of useability.

Command line interface (CLI)

The user interacts with the computer by typing in commands in response to prompts displayed on the screen.

👍 Experienced users find it quicker to complete tasks.

👍 Requires far less memory and processing power than GUIs to run.

👎 Requires knowledge of the specific commands for performing functions.

👎 Learning so many commands can be intimidating for inexperienced users.

```
C:\Windows\system32\cmd.exe
16/12/2010  12:57                    41 .gitconfig
24/02/2012  21:31      <DIR>            .idlerc
31/10/2011  02:08      <DIR>            .jdiskreport
21/05/2012  10:16      <DIR>            .VirtualBox
13/01/2012  00:13      <DIR>            Adobe Flash Builder 4.5
23/12/2010  13:32      <DIR>            Calibre Library
15/02/2012  20:46      <DIR>            Contacts
22/05/2012  16:49      <DIR>            Desktop
13/04/2012  10:06      <DIR>            Documents
19/03/2012  00:14      <DIR>            Downloads
15/02/2012  20:46      <DIR>            Favorites
07/12/2011  11:25                60,304 g2mdlhlpx.exe
15/02/2012  20:46      <DIR>            Links
15/02/2012  20:46      <DIR>            Music
16/04/2012  15:04      <DIR>            Pictures
15/02/2012  20:46      <DIR>            Saved Games
15/02/2011  04:23      <DIR>            Searches
15/02/2012  20:46                     0 Sti_Trace.log
15/02/2012  20:46      <DIR>            Videos
13/04/2011  04:13      <DIR>            Vir
              3 File(s)         60,349
             22 Dir(s)  821,324,812,28
```

Command line interfaces use a simple text-based screen to provide interaction.

Graphical user interface (GUI)

Users interact with the device by controlling a pointer or touch screen to select icons and menus displayed on screen. GUIs are widely used on devices from PCs to smartphones.

👍 This simple, intuitive method of interacting is easy for beginners to use.

👍 It doesn't require users to learn any commands to perform tasks.

👍 There are usually options to adapt the interface according to an individual user's needs, for example by using screen magnifiers or changing the colours or font sizes.

👎 It is often resource intensive, requiring a lot of processor power and memory.

👎 Experienced users can find it frustrating to complete tasks they could perform in a CLI with one command.

Menu based interface

Users interact using a simple menu that presents options to choose from. An example is an ATM screen.

👍 The limited number of options makes it easy to use.

👍 It is often possible to figure out how to perform tasks without any instruction.

👍 They can include options to adapt the interface for an individual user's needs, for example by providing speech output or a choice of larger font size.

👎 Performing tasks can be slow and frustrating where many levels of options must be traversed.

Tourist Information: Liverpool

Theatres	Cinemas	Museums
Pubs & restaurants	Shopping	Night life
Public transport	Ferries	Parking

Click to find out more!

Menu based interfaces offer simple options to provide interaction.

Now try this

Rahul is an expert user of computer systems and has spent many years using different types of operating system user interface.

Explain why Rahul is more suited to using a command line interface.

Make sure that you explain what it is about Rahul that makes a CLI advantageous for him.

Utility software

Utility software is used to manage system resources. Utilities are like a tool box to help us optimise and maintain our computer system. Many utilities are pre-installed as part of the operating system, such as traceroute, while others may be selected by the user and installed, such as anti-virus scanners.

Disk utilities

Disk utilities are designed to maintain the performance of a computer's disk drive.

File compressors – backing up very large files and sharing them online can be difficult. This utility compresses files to reduce their size and decompresses them for later access.

Backup – you regularly want to back up your files, but this can be slow as a manual process. Backup utilities allow you to automate the backup process.

Disk defragmenter – over time a computer's disk drive becomes fragmented, which slows down file access. This utility reorganises the data for quicker access, but is only required on a HDD when using Windows (fat32/NTFS) file systems.

Network utilities

Network utilities are designed to maintain good network traffic and keep networks secure.

Firewalls – open networks are at risk from threats like hackers and worms. Firewalls prevent unauthorised access by monitoring and blocking suspicious traffic.

Anti-virus – this utility prevents computers from receiving viruses and detects and removes viruses that have already infected a system.

Traceroute allows you to display the path that data packets travel over an IP network to help diagnose problems.

Other utilities

There is a huge range of utilities which do not fall under a particular category.

Registry cleaners are designed for Windows systems to remove old, redundant registry entries. This can help improve system performance.

System profilers display a detailed breakdown of the system, including hardware and software. This can help with deciding where a system needs upgrading and diagnosing problems with the system.

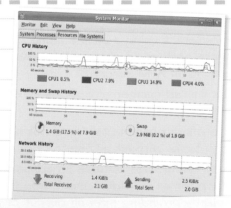

System monitors monitor resources and performance of PC systems. They help identify the causes of poor system performance.

Now try this

Jessica wants to improve the performance of her computer system as it has been running slowly recently.

Analyse the features of two utility tools that would help Jessica improve her system performance.

The question asks you to 'analyse' rather than simply 'explain'. Make sure you clearly explain why each feature you identify would be useful for Jessica and how they would therefore improve the system's performance. You should also comment on how effective they might be.

File types

Different file types are used to denote the form, or structure, of the data stored within the file. The file extension tells the user what type of data the file should contain. It also tells the operating system which icon to display and which software to use to open the file when the user double clicks the icon.

Examples of file types

GIF – small file size, but low quality due to limited number of colours. Can display basic transparency and animation.

JPG – good compression, although compression is lossy so files cannot be decompressed.

BMP – an uncompressed file format, so image quality is extremely high but file size is very large.

DOC and RTF – commonly used file formats for documents created using word processing software.

PDF – a format that represents data independently of the originating software and/or hardware.

Image file types

File types

Application software file types

XLS – a common format for files created using spreadsheet software.

PNG – uses lossless compression to save high-quality images in a low file size. Also allows transparency.

 For more on lossy and lossless compression, see page 20.

MDB and ACCDB – common file types for database software.

PPT – a common format for slideshows created using presentation software.

ODF – an open source XML based format used to represent office files such as spreadsheets, word processing, etc.

MKV – supports high-quality video playback but is not well supported by some devices, e.g. iPads can't play .mkv files.

Video file types

AVI – uncompressed so is very high quality but very large file size. Not good for streaming.

MOV – designed for use with Apple QuickTime software, but it can be played using other software. Can provide high quality but can also be compressed. Good for streaming.

MP4 – supports high-quality video while still compressing file size. Works on a wide variety of devices and software.

Implications of file types

The choice of file type or storage method of data has ongoing implications for individuals and organisations, including:

Issue	Description	Why might this be an issue?
Compatibility	Some file types only work with certain software.	May need to purchase new software. Sharing files with others who do not have the required software.
Quality	Different image, video and audio file types provide varying levels of quality.	Choice will depend on intended use of the files – e.g. is high quality the priority or small file size?
File size	The file type affects file size – some types are very efficient in the way they store data whereas others use lots of storage space.	File size may have implications for storing, transmitting or displaying files.

Now try this

Kasim is making a website to advertise his wedding photography business and wants to know what file type he should be using to display his photographs.

Explain the benefits of using two different file types for displaying his images.

 Think about the benefits of a jpg compared to a bmp or a gif.

Application software

Application software allows end users to complete tasks, such as creating a report or a presentation.

Uses of application software

There are many different types of application software that have their own uses. These include:

Productivity software – these are applications like word processors, desktop publishers and spreadsheets that are used in office environments to support business tasks and improve efficiency.

Graphics software – these applications are used to edit photos or create original artwork.

Communications software – these applications make communicating quicker and easier. They include instant messaging, email and VOIP software.

Proprietary and open source software

These terms refer to who owns the source code behind the software.

Proprietary software

The source code is privately owned by the software company.

Users pay to buy or subscribe to the software.

👍 Support (for example, for setup and troubleshooting) is provided by the software creators.

👍 It may have more features than open source software.

👎 The software company may be slow to provide updates and bug fixes.

👎 Software is usually very generic, with little scope for customisation due to copyright or complexity issues.

👎 It can be costly.

Open source software

The source code is available to read and modify.

👍 Most open source software is free to use, although many companies provide paid-for services to enhance and/or support open source.

👍 Support and fixes are provided by the community, often via forums.

👍 Open source utility software is usually compatible with other proprietary utility software.

👎 Support with fast response may not be available when needed, as it relies on good will.

👎 There may be indirect costs involved in paying for support and training.

Choosing software

When choosing software, consider:

- ease of use – familiarity and ease of use is paramount
- reliability – ensuring software works as intended and can be depended upon
- capability – that the software can do the job required of it and do it effectively.

Performance

When looking at performance, consider:

- the maturity of the software, as stable versions of software can be more efficient given there has been time for bugs to be resolved
- interoperability – interface with other devices or systems
- support of dedicated hardware for complex tasks.

Now try this

Seth is looking at different software options for managing orders and deliveries in his freight shipping business.

Analyse the relevant benefits and drawbacks to Seth of using an open source software application for meeting his needs.

This task requires greater depth as it asks for you to 'analyse'. Identify advantages and clearly explain why they would be useful for Seth, as well as how some drawbacks would affect him.

Emerging technologies

Emerging technologies are those that are currently in development and are just starting to make an impact on business and general society.

What are emerging technologies?

Some of the emerging technologies we see today include:

- artificial intelligence
- biometrics
- robotics
- virtual reality.

Virtual reality is an emerging technology set to make a big impact on how we entertain ourselves at home.

Emerging technologies at home and work

Emerging technologies are changing the way we live our personal lives and the way we do business. Here are some examples.

At home

Artificial intelligence in automated vacuum cleaners gives us more leisure time. Self-driving cars could soon make the roads safer.

Biometrics let us log securely into our tablets and smartphones through our thumb print.

Virtual reality is opening up new and exciting video gaming opportunities.

Domestic robots can carry out household chores or home security. Social robots provide companionship.

At work

Artificial intelligence used in business forecasts is helping in decision making

Biometrics are increasing security at airports through facial recognition at passport checks.

Robots are performing dangerous jobs without risk to life. They can then carry out routine production line tasks, as well as delicate surgical procedures.

Virtual reality is allowing businesses to test products under development in a virtual environment.

Implications of emerging technologies

- The Internet of Things (IoT) allows your car to know where you are going and how to get there, and your fridge to pre-order your supplies, but all this needs data. Increasingly, advanced data-hungry technologies are placing a strain on the existing infrastructure.
- Society demands data wherever and whenever it likes – we are no longer confined to the home WIFI network or the office LAN. Location-aware technologies and the availability of 3D imagery means that data access is essential to maintain and develop the emerging world of virtual reality and autonomous systems.
- There are new ways of gathering data resulting in the emergence of 'big data' which means we need new ways of analysing it.
- New ways of identifying ourselves through biometric data also brings the need for greater and more powerful security.

Now try this

Liam has a small chain of petrol stations and wants to capture the buying habits of his customers so he has introduced a loyalty card scheme.

Explain what other measures Liam needs to consider so he can get useful marketing information.

Think about how Liam is going to collect data and what he will do with it. Explain the potential impact on his existing systems.

Choosing an IT system

There are many factors to consider when choosing the best system for the end user, ranging from what the system needs to be capable of doing to how the user interacts with it and what devices make up the system.

User experience and needs

Does the user need the system to be always available, even when on the go?

Is the user experienced with computer systems or do they need a system that is easy to use?

Are they looking for performance, e.g. for video gaming, and need a system with a high specification graphics device?

Is accessibility an important issue?

Specifications, compatibility and connectivity

Does the system meet the specification requirements of the software to be used?

Will the system work with other devices?

Can the IT system use the required connectivity technology. e.g. for using mobile internet connections or syncing devices?

Cost

Does the user have a large budget, allowing you to choose components from well-known brands?

Do they have a small budget which requires looking for a cheaper alternative?

Efficiency and productivity

Is the efficiency of the system a key issue?

Do users need to be highly productive?

Is it essential that the system is able to start up fast, load and save programs and files quickly, never stutter or crash or have any other problems?

Does the user have the budget for the higher-end machines that provide greater efficiency?

Implementation

What is the timescale for the IT system to be implemented?

Does the system need to be available quickly?

Will the system need extensive testing?

Will you need to migrate data from an old system to the new one?

Will users need training in order to use the system?

Security

Will the system be handling sensitive information?

Does it need biometric security for login or the ability to attach physical security such as locks?

Are portable devices not appropriate because of the risk of them being stolen?

Now try this

Fraser has asked his friend Benjamin to advise him on a new IT system for playing high-end online video games.

Look through all the factors listed on the page. When you have chosen the two you think are most important, make sure you explain their relevance to the case study.

Explain two factors that Benjamin has to consider when choosing an IT system for Fraser.

Wired connection methods

Wired methods of connecting devices are any method that uses physical cables to connect between devices, systems or components. Different types of connection rely on widely differing connectors, depending on what the signal or data is transmitting.

Wired system connection methods

	Uses	Advantages	Limitations
Cat5	Telephone communications and ethernet networks.	👍 Versatile and widely available. 👍 Cheap compared to other networking options.	👎 Only useful over shorter distances. 👎 More susceptible to interference than other wired techniques such as fibre.
Coaxial	All types of data communication, commonly used in television cabling.	👍 Less susceptible to interference than UTP/STP so works over longer distances. 👍 Cheap, though not as cheap as UTP/STP.	👎 Thickness of cable makes it difficult to work with. 👎 Limited bandwidth.
Fibre optic	Telephone and internet cables, cable television and computer networking.	👍 Improved security as the cable cannot be tapped. 👍 Can be used over long distances. 👍 High data transfer rate.	👎 Very expensive. 👎 Specialist skills needed to install.

Wired device connections

	Uses	Advantages	Limitations
VGA	Analogue connection of video display equipment, such as projectors, CRTs or LCDs.	👍 Universally used on high-resolution display equipment. 👍 Low-cost cabling.	👎 Cumbersome cabling. 👎 Signal affected over distance (noise). 👎 No DRM (digital rights management).
HDMI	Digital connection of both video and sound from devices to display equipment.	👍 Capable of 8k (and beyond) resolution. 👍 Used in computing and entertainment.	👎 Limited length. 👎 Cabling and technology is more expensive than analogue equivalents such as VGA.
USB/ FireWire	Connecting equipment and peripherals, such as printers, scanners, input devices, cameras.	👍 High speed capability. 👍 Backwards compatibility. 👍 Can connect multiple devices.	👎 Limited distance. 👎 Limited power supply.

Now try this

Meera wants to connect her new laptop to the large 4k LCD Touchscreen TV in the conference room to allow her to collaborate with colleagues on product development.

Describe what wired connection methods Meera should consider to get the best out of the system.

Make sure you consider ALL aspects of connecting the screen to Meera's computing equipment and how she might make use of the display as both an input and an output device.

Wireless connection methods

Wireless connection methods connect using the electromagnetic spectrum. This may be traditional radio waves or even light waves.

Wireless system connection methods

	Uses	Advantages	Limitations
WiFi	To connect devices wirelessly to local and wide area networks such as the internet.	👍 High data transfer speeds. 👍 Good range. 👍 Relatively cheap to install.	👎 Can be complex. 👎 Security concerns.
3G/4G/ WiMAX	To connect to data networks such as the internet whilst on the move.	👍 Allows true mobility. 👍 4G provides for very fast connection speeds.	👎 Heavy data usage can be costly. 👎 Uses public networks.
Satellite broadband	Provides connectivity to remote areas, often rural.	👍 Wide coverage. 👍 High speed.	👎 High latency. 👎 Subject to weather conditions.
Microwave/ Laser	Allows point-to-point LAN connections between locations.	👍 High speed. 👍 No ongoing costs.	👎 Affected by poor weather. 👎 High initial cost.

Wireless connections methods for devices

	Uses	Advantages	Limitations
Bluetooth	For pairing devices over short distances, such as wireless headphones, watches, keyboards and mice.	👍 Easy to set up. 👍 Low power consumption.	👎 Low data transfer speeds. 👎 Very short range.
WiFi Direct	For connecting devices to remote displays.	👍 Can transmit both audio and video. 👍 Usually built in to devices.	👎 Limited range. 👎 Can affect data connectivity (interference).
WiFi	Allows 'ad-hoc' networks to permit wireless printing/ scanning, for example.	👍 Simple setup. 👍 Uses existing WiFi infrastructure.	👎 Using ad-hoc networks can impact connectivity.

Now try this

Shaheera wants to set up a local area network in her home to allow her to share an internet connection and files between her different devices.

Explain two benefits of using WiFi for her home network.

Make sure you compare WiFi to other methods of connecting Shaheera's devices, both cabled and other wireless methods.

Features of different networks

Different types of network can be defined by their size (personal, local, wide area networks) or by their purpose (virtual private networks).

Local area networks (LAN) and wide area networks (WAN)

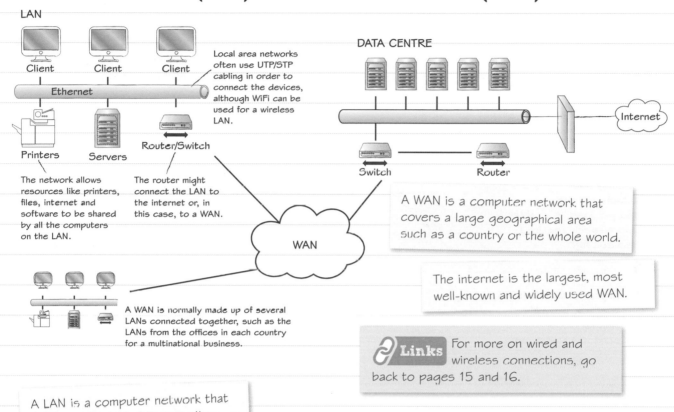

LAN

Client   Client   Client

Ethernet

Printers   Servers   Router/Switch

Local area networks often use UTP/STP cabling in order to connect the devices, although WiFi can be used for a wireless LAN.

DATA CENTRE

Switch   Router   Internet

The network allows resources like printers, files, internet and software to be shared by all the computers on the LAN.

The router might connect the LAN to the internet or, in this case, to a WAN.

WAN

A WAN is a computer network that covers a large geographical area such as a country or the whole world.

The internet is the largest, most well-known and widely used WAN.

A WAN is normally made up of several LANs connected together, such as the LANs from the offices in each country for a multinational business.

Links For more on wired and wireless connections, go back to pages 15 and 16.

A LAN is a computer network that covers a single building or site.

Personal area network (PAN)

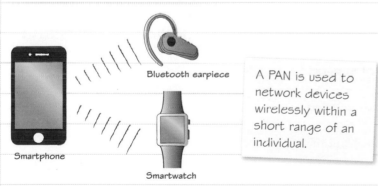

Bluetooth earpiece

Smartphone

Smartwatch

A PAN is used to network devices wirelessly within a short range of an individual.

Bluetooth is commonly used to create a PAN to connect all the digital devices in a person's workspace, for example connecting a mobile phone to a Bluetooth headset for hands-free operation.

Virtual private network (VPN)

This network technology creates a secure network connection over a public network, usually the internet, by using encryption.

This allows a business to have a secure wide area network without having to pay the high costs of constructing the physical network infrastructure, as they can use the existing internet infrastructure.

Links For a diagram of a VPN, see page 20.

Now try this

James is considering whether he should use his home's wireless network or use Bluetooth to allow him to connect his PC, smartphone, printer and smartwatch.

Explain what the differences are in terms of the type of network (PAN, LAN and WAN) and what he should consider when making his decision.

Make sure you cover three different factors and link them to the features of PANs and LANs.

Network choice and performance

Networks are all around us and are as unique as the users who use them. There are many factors and reasons for selecting the various components that make up a network.

Factors affecting choice of network

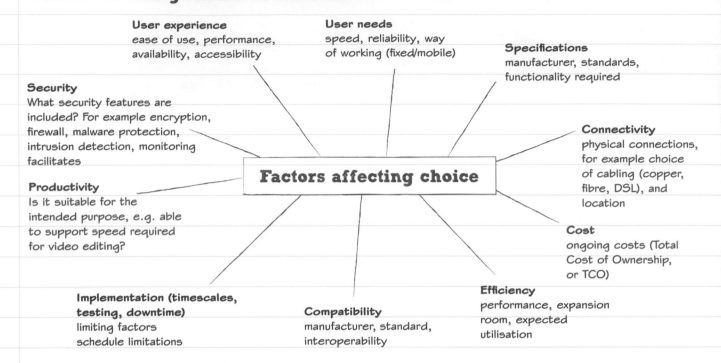

User experience
ease of use, performance, availability, accessibility

User needs
speed, reliability, way of working (fixed/mobile)

Specifications
manufacturer, standards, functionality required

Security
What security features are included? For example encryption, firewall, malware protection, intrusion detection, monitoring facilitates

Connectivity
physical connections, for example choice of cabling (copper, fibre, DSL), and location

Productivity
Is it suitable for the intended purpose, e.g. able to support speed required for video editing?

Factors affecting choice

Cost
ongoing costs (Total Cost of Ownership, or TCO)

Implementation (timescales, testing, downtime)
limiting factors schedule limitations

Compatibility
manufacturer, standard, interoperability

Efficiency
performance, expansion room, expected utilisation

Choosing components

Consider:

- manufacturer – is there an affinity to a particular manufacturer? What is the corporate policy?
- specification – what kit meets the needs and supports required features?
- warranty/ongoing support – corporate level of support? SLA? Response times?
- adherence to standards – will it work well with existing components?
- familiarity – are there specific skills that in-house staff possess?
- infrastructure – what does it have to fit into, e.g. incorporate existing Cat6 cabling?

Performance factors

Consider:

- available bandwidth and connection methods
- load – is the demand likely to be 100% loading the components (how much 'wiggle room' is there)?
- professional level equipment or SOHO equipment?
- infrastructure – is it being used on ageing infrastructure?

Now try this

Jane's graphic design business is expanding and she is recruiting two new graphic artists and moving into a small unit.

Explain two factors Jane should consider when choosing a network infrastructure.

Don't forget to think about the future. How might Jane's business continue to grow and what impact might this have?

Protocols

Protocols are the rules that define methods of communicating data between two or more digital devices. They ensure that the transmission of data always follows a set procedure. There are different protocols for different applications.

TCP/IP

Transmission Control Protocol and Internet Protocol are used together as the basic communication language of the internet.

Data sent over the internet is broken up into 'packets' to enable it to be sent more efficiently. Each packet is sent individually and then re-assembled at the destination.

- TCP is used to create the packets and reassemble them at the end.
- IP is used to route packets to the intended computer, using the computer's IP address.

 Links Have a look at the diagram of the TCP/IP stack on page 8.

Email

SMTP – the Simple Mail Transfer Protocol is used to transfer emails between mail servers. It is also used to transfer email from the client software to the outgoing mail server.

POP3 – the Post Office Protocol 3 is used to retrieve emails from the mail server. It allows us to download messages to our client software for offline reading.

IMAP – the Internet Message Access Protocol is used to retrieve emails from the mail server. Rather than downloading the messages, IMAP syncs them with the mail server.

Voice and video calls

Many companies use their own proprietary protocols for voice and video calls over the internet. Some well-known protocols are:

H.323 – this was one of the first successful VOIP protocols and is recommended by the ITU (International Telecommunication Union). It defines the rules for communicating audio and video over packet switched networks.

SIP – the Session Initiation Protocol is used to create, control and end VOIP connections.

RTP – the Real-time Transport Protocol is designed to transfer audio and video over IP-based networks.

Web pages

HTTP – the HyperText Transfer Protocol is used to allow web servers and browsers to transfer files over the Internet. It is how we access the World Wide Web.

HTTPS – the secure version of the standard HTTP. It uses public key cryptography to encrypt communications between a web browser and server.

FTP – the File Transfer Protocol is used to transfer files over a network. It is the technology used to upload files to a server as well as to download large files.

Security protocols

SSL (Secure Sockets Layer) and **TLS** (Transport Layer Security) are used to ensure that transactions over networks are kept safe. SSL is gradually being phased out and replaced with TLS.

Now try this

Alex is a business executive who uses email as her main means of communication. As she has to travel a lot she needs to use her email on several different devices.

Evaluate the protocols used for receiving emails and which would be most beneficial to Alex.

There are two protocols to talk about for this question. Look at the case study – one protocol is certainly more useful to Alex than the other. Remember, when you are asked to 'evaluate', you need to review the information so you can give a supported judgement about the topic or problem. Often, a conclusion will be required.

Data transmission issues

Data transmission is an important part of computer use. It involves sending digital messages between devices in a network, such as in a LAN or over the internet. Here are the main issues associated with data transmission that you need to know about.

Security considerations

User authentication – usernames and passwords authenticate users who have permission to use a network and prevent unauthorised access by hackers.

Firewalls – these monitor traffic to prevent unauthorised access and dangerous data packets being passed into the system and causing harm.

Encryption – information can be intercepted while being transmitted. Using encryption ensures intercepted data cannot be read. HTTPS is a commonly used method for secure data transmission.

VPNs and security

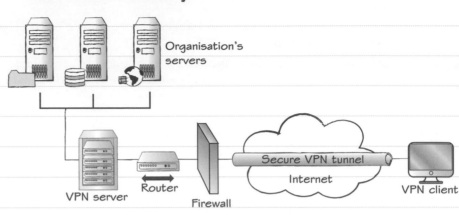

VPNs create a secure connection between remote sites and users over the internet to prevent data being intercepted and read.

Bandwidth and latency

Bandwidth is the rate of data transfer over a network – usually measured in bits per second.

Latency is the time delay for a data packet to transfer to its destination – usually measured in milliseconds.

Bandwidth and latency implications

Browsing the internet doesn't need an instant response so latency isn't a big factor. Bandwidth is an important factor as it affects how long files take to download.

Online gaming needs very low latency as players need a fast response for real-time updates of character movements, etc.

Video calls need low latency and high bandwidth as you need to transfer a lot of data (video and audio), but you also want a fast response to avoid stutter.

Compression

Compression reduces file size so files can be transferred faster. Compression is used for images to be displayed on the Web, video and audio in streaming and VOIP, and documents attached to emails. There are two main types of compression.

- **Lossy** – data removed during compression is permanently deleted. Commonly used in images, audio and video.
- **Lossless** – all original data can be recovered when uncompressed. Commonly used for documents.

Codecs

A codec is a program used to compress and decompress video and audio files. This reduces the space they take up on disk and allows fast transfer over a network, such as the internet, for VOIP calls and online streaming.

This leads to a loss of quality in the video or audio – in the resolution, frames per second or both.

Now try this

Joanna is a big fan of online video games. She is currently experiencing a lot of skipping. She has a high bandwidth connection and thinks the problem is the latency.

Describe how bandwidth and latency would affect Joanna when playing video games.

Make sure you relate your answer to the context of video gaming.

Features of online systems

Cloud storage is a method of storage where data is stored on remote servers, rather than on the user's local computer or in an organisation's own data centre. Similarly, in cloud computing, software is stored on remote servers and accessed by users via their browser.

Uses of ...

cloud storage

Personal use

- Storing files such as photos and videos online, so they are synced and accessible on all the user's devices.

Professional use

- Storing off-site backups of business data, to allow recovery in case of loss of data.
- Accessing business documents while working off-site.

cloud computing

Personal use

- Accessing graphics editing software, email and home office software on a variety of home computing devices.

Professional use

- Accessing office applications and email without having to install the software on all workstations.

The impact of cloud storage and computing ...

on individuals

on organisations

Advantages
👍 Data can be accessed on the wide variety of devices used in the home.
👍 Software with specification requirements that are too high for a home computer can be easily accessed through cloud computing.

Disadvantages
👎 Cloud storage and computing can make heavy use of bandwidth.
👎 Hackers could access and misuse personal photos or videos on the cloud storage servers.

Advantages
👍 Off-site backups are more physically secure (e.g safe from fire).
👍 A business can subscribe and unsubscribe to software according to changing needs.
👍 Organisations can save money as IT staff are not needed to manage software installations and less powerful hardware is required.

Disadvantages
👎 Organisations have no control over the security of their backups, as that is controlled by the cloud storage company.
👎 Privacy concerns over who can access the organisation's data within the cloud storage company.
👎 Software is inaccessible if there is a network outage.

Now try this

Kyle uses his smartphone to take photos and videos which he normally stores on his device. He has a mobile 3G internet connection, and he has decided he would like to use cloud storage to save his photos and videos so he can instantly access them on his PC when he gets home.

Note that Kyle is using a mobile internet connection. What are some of the issues with this that could impact on uploading videos to cloud storage?

Explain two implications of using cloud storage for Kyle.

Using online systems

Using online systems, such as cloud computing and storage, can offer big benefits to organisations and individuals. However, there are factors that must be considered before switching to these online systems to ensure it is the best decision for an organisation.

1 Security

Online systems create security concerns as data is accessible over the internet, potentially to hackers, and you have little control over security procedures.

If security is important, choose an organisation that implements high security protocols.

2 Cost

There is a great range in the costs for online services. Many cloud storage services are free of charge to individual users up to a certain data limit, but charge monthly fees for businesses.

There are free services available to organisations, which can save a lot of money, such as Google Drive (although if you want to impose things like corporate control and policies, costs are involved).

4 Features

Cloud software sometimes has fewer features than a locally installed version. However there are a wide range of options available, as cloud services allow users a lot of choice to find a suitable product.

3 Ease of use

Some online services are easier for non-technical users than others. Cloud storage systems often sync your data with your computer, allowing you to access your cloud files using the same interface as for your local files.

Also check on the amount of technical support available to users.

5 Connectivity

Cloud-based storage and software require internet connections in order to access the services.

You may be limited in your options if your internet connection is slow or you have a limited data allowance.

Remote working

Online systems allow people working from home, or anywhere outside the office site, to access the network of the organisation they work for. Systems that help with this include:

- **VPN** – allows a secure connection to be made to the organisation's network over the internet.

- **Remote desktop technology** can also be used to fix computer problems remotely, and is often used by technical support departments to promote a more effective way of working.

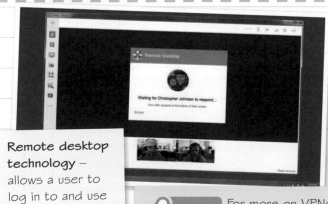

Remote desktop technology – allows a user to log in to and use their work system from a remote device.

🔗 **Links** For more on VPNs, see pages 17 and 20.

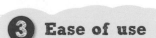 **Now try this**

Kasia is looking into switching to a cloud-based office software service for her small business.

Explain two factors that Kasia must consider before switching to an online service.

Always read the question carefully. Make sure your answers are relevant to cloud software and not cloud storage.

Online communities: methods of communicating

An online community is a group of people who communicate over the internet about common interests. We use a wide variety of different online services to form and participate in these online communities.

Here are six commonly used types of online community.

 Social media

Social media sites like Facebook are used to share content and communicate with others. A key part of this is creating groups, often based around locations, events or hobbies, to communicate news and stories with others who share these interests. There are also professional media sites, such as LinkedIn.

 Blog

Blogs, microblogs (snippets of information rather than longer posts) and vlogs (video blogs) let people regularly share information, such as news and opinions, with others on a topic of interest.

Others can then comment on the videos or blog posts to create a dialogue between people with shared interests.

 Wiki

Wikis are created and maintained by online communities. Groups of people with shared interests add and edit content on a site to ensure the information is up to date and accurate.

For example, you can find a dedicated wiki for most popular video games, movies and TV shows.

 Chatroom/instant messaging

- A chatroom is a website where users can communicate by posting short text messages. These are viewable by everyone on the chatroom.

- Instant messaging also lets users write short text messages but directly to a person or a group of selected people, so it is slightly more private.

 Podcasts

Podcasts are audio (and sometimes video) files posted to the internet for download. They are normally produced as a series on a particular topic. People interested in the topic can subscribe to the podcast to get the latest episode.

 Forums

Also known as a message board, a forum is a website used for online discussion where users can post messages and questions publicly for other users of the site to read and respond to.

Forums are usually based on a topic of interest, such as technology or particular hobbies.

Now try this

Amit is a big fan of football and wants to be able to chat with others about his favourite team.

Describe three different methods for Amit to get involved in an online community.

There are lots of different options here. Make sure you mention examples of how Amit would use each type of online community you identify.

Online communities: implications

Both individuals and organisations make extensive use of online communities. This has had many implications on how we live our lives and how we work. Many are positive but some are negative.

Implications of online communities for individuals and organisations

Privacy
- Personal information accessible by other users.
- Can be misused by others, such as for cyberbullying.

Cost
- Usually free for users to make use of.
- Users need to accept advertising.

Meeting needs
- Allows users to communicate with others, organise events, etc.

User experience
- Ease of use – services often offer sophisticated features but are nevertheless intuitive and accessible.
- Accessibility – can provide companionship for individuals isolated due to a disability or other personal circumstances.
- Performance – can be used on a range of devices effectively. A lot of communities have dedicated apps to target lower powered devices
- Availability – being able to use offline or with limited connectivity is a challenge.

Security
- Danger of accounts being hacked and data stolen.
- Information could be used for identity and bank fraud.

For individuals

IMPLICATIONS OF ONLINE COMMUNITIES

For organisations

Customer needs
- Communicating with customers is easier.
- Easier communication helps a business understand customer needs better.

Cost
- Maintaining a presence through online communities is usually cost free, although additional paid for services are available (for example direct marketing).
- Implementing own system has large development costs.

Security
- Systems vulnerable to hacking attempts, which may result in damage to reputation and image, as well as potential legal issues.
- IT security staff and procedures required.

Employee/customer experience
- Improves their experience of a business due to good communication.

Current systems
- May need to transfer data from existing systems.
- May need to communicate with existing systems.

Productivity
- Can cause distractions for employees.
- Can improve communication which can aid productivity.

Implementation
- Extensive testing needed to ensure no errors.
- Timescales may be long for implementing system.

Working practices
- Changes the way we work.
- New job roles for social media and new advertising opportunities.

Now try this

A business is considering implementing a forum to provide customer support and to allow customers to feed back on products.

Explain two impacts for the organisation of implementing a forum.

Try to think of both positive and negative implications for the business.

You aren't asked to make a recommendation for the business, but bear in mind what you might recommend if this was an 'analyse' question.

Threats to data, information and systems

Using information technology systems to store and transmit information in digital form always comes with threats to the security and privacy of the data being used.

1 Malware

This is software designed to cause harm to your IT system, such as deleting, altering or stealing data.

2 Hackers

A person who exploits weaknesses in IT systems in order to gain unauthorised access is known as a hacker. This can be done to steal, alter and delete data from your system. (There are also 'ethical hackers' who are employed by companies to test defences and security.)

3 Phishing

A phishing email is one that pretends to be from a reputable company in order to get individuals to reveal personal information.

4 Accidental damage

Not all threats to individuals and businesses are malicious.

A lot of damage is caused through human error, such as accidentally deleting or overwriting files on a computer, or spilling a drink on a device and damaging it.

Examples of threats to data and systems

> Viruses, worms, trojans and spyware are all examples of malware.

Remedy FREE edition virus software

🔍 **Threat Detected!**

While opening file: C\Documents and Settings\Emma\Desktop\MusicMan.EXE
Trojan horse BreakOut.Feralpoint8.PUM

[?] [Ignore] [Info] [Heal] [Move to vault]

✳ RELY Bank

Dear Sir/Madam,

We would like to notify you that an attempt has been made, within a country other than the UK, to withdraw the amount of €560.00 from your account.

If you did not make this withdrawal, someone else may have gained access to your account, and we need to verify your personal details. Please click on the link below to report this withdrawal as incorrect and to confirm your personal details.

We aim to resolve any discrepancies within 10 days.

Thank you for choosing to bank with RelyBank.

Member FDIC ©2010 RelyBank Ltd

> A common **phishing** email claims to be from a bank. It instructs the user to click on a link and enter their bank details, supposedly for verification purposes, but really to steal the person's bank details.

The impact of threats on individuals and organisations

The impact on individuals	The impact on organisations
• **Identity fraud** – the stolen personal information is used to open bank accounts, obtain loans, take out mobile phone contracts, etc. • **Bank fraud** – a criminal user gains access to your bank account and uses it to withdraw cash and purchase items.	• **Loss of reputation** – a business affected by any of the issues will lose the confidence of customers, who will turn to other businesses that haven't been affected. • **Loss of income** – during the down time caused by many of these threats, a business will not be able to carry out its normal business practices.

Now try this

Henley Investments is a finance company that provides investment advice and financial portfolio management services. Given the sensitive nature of the financial information that the firm manages using IT systems, it is concerned about threats to its systems.

Analyse the impact that threats to data security might have on Henley investments.

> You need to fully describe each threat you identify and examine its potential impact on Henley Investments.

Protecting data: tools and techniques

There are many tools and techniques we can use for protecting data stored and transferred using IT systems. Software and hardware tools are one important approach, as well as techniques and processes for limiting access and securing data.

Techniques for protecting data

File permissions and access levels
Ensure access is restricted to those who need it.

Backup and recovery procedures
Ensure that data can be recovered following any loss of data.

Passwords
Limit access by ensuring users keep a secure password to access system.

Protecting data

Protocols
Define data transfer processes to ensure secure transfer.

Digital certificates
Allow secure data transfer using public key encryption.

Physical access control
Prevent unauthorised access using locks, biometrics, etc.

Biometric authentification identifies individuals' unique fingerprint patterns.

Tools for protecting data

Tool	Description	Reason for using	Need to be aware of
1 Anti-virus software	Detects and removes viruses and other malware from a computer system.	Protects systems from all forms of malware.	Must be regularly updated as new viruses are created regularly.
2 Firewalls	Monitor network traffic into and out of an IT system; block suspicious traffic to prevent unauthorised access.	Firewalls are key in preventing hacking attempts as well as worms.	Firewalls are not 100% effective – security holes can be exploited, e.g. in outdated software.
3 Encryption	The conversion of data into an unreadable code known as ciphertext.	The most effective form of security, as encrypted data cannot be read without the encryption key.	Encryption keys must be maintained and kept secure. A lost key means the data is irretrievable.

Encryption of stored and transmitted data

- We encrypt our hard disk so that anyone who gains access to our system (a hacker, or someone accessing a stolen device) cannot read our stored data.
- We encrypt data while it is being transmitted so that if it is intercepted it cannot be read.

Now try this

Highcastle Advertising is an advertising agency that works with companies requiring high levels of security for their new products.

Analyse two techniques that Highcastle Advertising can use to keep their data secure.

As well as naming and describing the techniques, identify how each one protects the data and the implications it has for Highcastle Advertising.

Protecting data: legislation and codes of practice

Data protection is supported through legislation. Non-compliance is very serious and can be punished with large fines and imprisonment.

Legislation for protecting data

The main data protection laws are the Data Protection Act and the Computer Misuse Act.

	Role	Impact on organisations	Impact on individuals
Data Protection Act 1998	• The main UK legislation for protection of personal data. • Protects the privacy of individuals' personal data held by others. • Gives rights to individuals on what data is collected and how their data is used.	• Increased costs to meet requirements for data security. • Limited in how much data can be gathered and how it is used. • Fines of up to £500000 if in breach of the law.	• Personal data collected by others is likely to be kept secure and not be misused. • Compensation can be claimed for any harm caused due to misuse of an individual's data.
Computer Misuse Act 1990	• Protects against attacks on IT systems used to gain unauthorised access and steal or cause damage to data. • Covers threats like hacking and spreading malware.	• Organisations' computer systems are more secure due to the deterrent of legal repercussions for attacks on systems. • Requires organisations (and their employees) to develop and adhere to effective security policies.	• Provides protection from attacks to an individual's computer systems. • Those who carry out attacks can face unlimited fines and up to 10 years in prison.

Links For more on legislation associated with IT systems, see pages 38 and 39.

When data protection fails

In 2007, families in the UK were informed of a potentially massive fraud alert. This happened after two computer discs which held the personal details of all UK families with a child under 16 went missing.

The Child Benefit data included name, address, date of birth, National Insurance number and, in some cases, bank details of 25 million people and 7.25 million families.

On behalf of the government, the then chancellor, Alastair Darling, issued an apology and an emergency statement in which the incident was described as a 'catastrophic' failure.

Codes of practice

Professional bodies and the Information Commissioner's Office (ICO) define codes of practice for how organisations handle, share and protect data.

Codes of practice are not legal requirements – they are best practice guidelines, which aim to:

• help support compliance with the Data Protection Act, Computer Misuse Act and other related legislation.

• ensure data is not mishandled, which would lead to a negative impact on an organisation's reputation

• give individuals confidence that the data they supply to organisations will be safe.

Now try this

Susan is completing a registration form to sign up for an online retail site. In the process she is providing a variety of personal information to the business gathering the data.

Describe how two pieces of legislation help to protect Susan's data.

Make sure you name each piece of legislation before you describe it. Identify an impact of each law on Susan's situation.

Features of online services

Online services are information and services that are made available over the internet, usually via a web browser. As a result, access to these services is extremely flexible and convenient.

Examples of online services

Some features are common to all types of online services. These include 24/7 access and availability on a wide range of devices. Others are more specific to different types of service.

1 Retail
- E-commerce sites
- Online auctions

👍 Wide range of competition to choose from.
👍 Saves transport time and costs.
👍 Better targeted marketing can be performed online.

👎 Products and services may not be regulated.
👎 May result in nuisance emails and texts.

2 Financial services
- Online banking
- Online trading

👍 Can manage finances from home.
👍 Reduces the need for visiting financial institutions to conduct business, resulting in reduced travel times and costs.

👎 Not all services may be genuine.
👎 Potential for unauthorised access through security breaches and social engineering.

3 Education and training
- Distance learning degrees
- E-learning new skills

👍 Can learn in your own time.
👍 Access to a wider range of courses than those taught in the local area.

👎 Need to make sure the course is properly accredited.
👎 Lack of structure may impede learning.

4 News and information
- Traffic reports
- Weather reports
- News websites

👍 Provides the most up-to-date information possible.
👍 Helps to plan travel and events to avoid traffic, bad weather, etc.
👍 Can be personalised to show news on particular topics.

👎 Need to check the reliability of the information provider.
👎 Too much information is accessible too quickly, for example potential impact and prejudgment of the accused before trial.

5 Entertainment and leisure
- Music/video streaming
- Online gaming

👍 Access to a wide range of music, TV and films for low subscription cost.
👍 Can play games with people all around the world.

👎 Safety locks may be needed to protect children from unsuitable content.

6 Productivity
- Cloud computing software
- Communication tools (e.g. video conferencing, email)

👍 Accessible anywhere with an internet connection and on most connected devices.
👍 Supports collaborative working, sharing information and communication.

👎 Potential for the loss of the 'human touch' by using technology to communicate and plan in isolation.

7 Booking systems
- Transport
- Hotels
- Appointments

👍 No need to travel to make booking.
👍 Fewer admin staff needed to take bookings.
👍 Avoids having to wait in a telephone queue (e.g. for GP appointment).

👎 May disadvantage those without internet access.

Now try this

Analyse the implications of different online services.

Not all implications are positive. In your answer to an 'analyse' question you'll be expected to discuss both the positives and negatives.

Business uses of online services

Some of the business uses of online services are collaborative working, the collection of transactional data and targeted marketing.

Collaborative working online

Online services such as cloud computing and VOIP allow people to collaborate on projects over the internet.

☑ Users in different locations can work on the same project.

☑ Users do not need to travel to work together, saving money, time and the environment.

☑ Users can work on the same document instead of on different versions.

☑ Users can use shared workspaces even though geographically separate.

Version control

This is important because it means a user knows which is the most up-to-date document to use. It is especially important when using collaborative working.

Version control can be managed by:

- locking the file and making it 'read only' while one user is viewing or editing it
- using software that allocates version numbers and dates of editing.

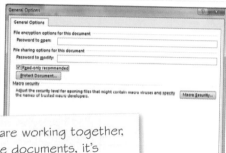

When people are working together, using the same documents, it's important to know you are using the most up-to-date version of a file or folder.

Transactional data

Businesses collect data from transactions made by their customers.

Examples of online transactions are purchases from retail sites and use of banking services.

Loyalty cards allow collection of data from purchases made in store as well as online. Cookies are used to track browsing habits and target advertising.

Uses of transactional data

Transactional data can be used to:

- ensure specific marketing
- analyse trends so that there is enough stock available to meet forecasts
- plan the workforce (particularly for service industries).

Targeted marketing

- This is used to target specific demographics, such as a particular age, gender or shared interest groups.
- It uses 'likes' to tailor marketing.
- It is relevant to recent search or browsing activity.

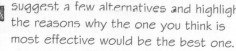

£10 OFF When you spend £30 or more

Businesses can use targeted marketing to reach very specific groups or even individuals.

Now try this

Meera produces customised gifts for all sorts of celebrations and is hoping to be able to concentrate on this full time.

Describe how Meera might use online services most effectively to increase her orders?

For questions like this you should suggest a few alternatives and highlight the reasons why the one you think is most effective would be the best one.

Uses and implications of IT systems

IT systems have been developed for use in many different ways by different types of organisation and business. Their impact is far-reaching in all areas of work.

Organisational uses and implications of IT systems

The table gives examples of uses of IT systems in organisations and some typical implications of those systems on the organisations using them.

IT system	Features and implications
1 Stock control	👍 Automatic stock reordering. 👍 Accurate stock levels recorded. 👎 Can be expensive and may require staff training.
2 Data logging and analysis	👍 Highly accurate recordings. 👍 Doesn't require humans to log data. 👍 Automatic processing of data and output in different formats. 👎 Requires persistent data connectivity to provide real time telemetry
3 General office tasks	👍 Improves efficiency and quality, e.g. in reports, presentations, spreadsheets. 👎 May require training of staff. 👎 IT support teams needed to correct issues and maintain software.
4 Creative tasks	👍 Makes it easier to edit film, music and artwork. 👍 Many ways of sharing creative work, e.g. video and image sharing websites. 👎 Files from creative tasks such as film editing require large storage capacities. 👎 Piracy concerns.
5 Online advertising	👍 Allows very specific targeted marketing based on users' browsing habits. 👍 Very cost effective, with a variety of payment methods, such as cost-per-click, cost-per-impression and cost-per-lead. 👎 Difficult to choose the best site for your adverts from the huge choice.
6 Manufacturing	👍 Improved efficiency – robots don't take breaks or make mistakes. 👍 Hazardous tasks can be performed by machinery. 👎 Loss of jobs in manufacturing, and can be very expensive to implement. 👎 Cannot deal with exceptions easily.
7 Security	👍 Includes technologies such as swipe cards and biometrics. 👍 CCTV monitoring and video technologies require fewer staff patrolling. 👎 Often expensive to implement these security systems due to the use of specialist hardware and often bespoke software solutions. 👎 Privacy concerns.

> Data logging systems can be used in hazardous conditions or places humans cannot access, for example geolocators to log the path of migrating birds.

Now try this

> Don't forget to look specifically at what impact your suggestions might have on Lisa's business and why.

Lisa runs a small cake company that specialises in bespoke cakes for both personal and corporate customers. At the moment, she doesn't use computers at all and estimates the cost of each cake.

Describe two ways that Lisa could use IT systems to help her develop her business.

Impact of IT systems on organisations

The potential of IT systems to enhance and improve businesses is obvious but there are many things to consider before embarking on the introduction of new IT systems in any organisation.

Impact of IT systems

User experience – does technology enhance what the users already do?

- Will it be easy to use and intuitive?
- Will the system increase performance and be reliable and available as users expect?
- What about users with additional needs?

Employee/customer needs – are people more productive and feel that the technology is helping them (or hindering them)?

- Losing touch – are businesses losing that personal touch in the quest for ever more efficient working?
- Big Brother – do customers and employees feel 'monitored' in a negative way?

Cost – how much is it going to cost, can this be related to the benefit received?

- Ongoing costs – maintenance, redundant systems
- People costs – training, skilled technical personnel

Implementation – how long might it take to put into place? How is the 'changeover' going to happen?

- Timescales and downtime – how long is it going to take? Is there a Plan B? How is downtime of existing systems (ways of working) going to be minimised?
- Testing – how is the system going to be tested thoroughly? Who is testing and how?

Replacement/integration with current systems – where does a system fit into the bigger picture?

- Will it work with existing systems?
- What about existing data? Customer records, sales records, financial records

Productivity – how does a system help a business meet its goals more effectively?

- Automation – reduce 'human error', increase efficiency

Working practices – what impact will it have on ways of working, people, processes?

User support and staff training needs (initial and ongoing) – is there a cost to train and upskill staff?

- Staff culture – how will staff accept new IT systems?
- Staff skillsets – does the level of technical and support expertise required change?

Security – how is sensitive data protected? Is it secure?

- Compliance with new legislation
- Public relations risk of data breaches

Now try this

Ayisha has a business operating three supermarkets. She is looking at how she can use ICT in order to make the running of the supermarkets more efficient, as well as how to expand her business.

Describe two potential uses of online services to help Ayisha achieve her goals and describe how they might impact other areas of the business.

When describing a use don't forget to include how a potential service might be implemented and use the checklist above to identify other stakeholders.

Gathering data

Organisations need to gather data for a wide variety of reasons. One of the most common reasons is to find out what their customers want and what they are prepared to buy.

Sources of data

When gathering data we can collect it from two different sources. These are:

- **Primary** – data is gathered directly from the source, for example using a survey or from sensor readings.

- **Secondary** – this is data that already exists, for example from previous research, books, journals or reports. It could also be data on shopping trends (bought from a market research company).

Data reliability

For data to be useful, it must be reliable. For data to be judged reliable it must be:

- Complete – all the data must be there. For example, sales data that misses a month's results could lead to incorrect decisions.

- Accurate – the data must be correct and truthful. This is easier to achieve from primary sources; secondary data must be from a trustworthy source.

Collecting primary data

Here are three common ways of carrying out a survey.

Surveys are an excellent method of gathering primary data. The organisation gathers the data itself, so can be sure it is reliable.

1 Questionnaire

This comprises a series of questions, usually close-ended with checkbox answer options. Traditional paper formats or electronic questionnaire websites can be used.

👍 Allows you to gather information from a large audience in a short space of time.

👍 All respondents get asked the same questions, giving consistency to data.

👎 The traditional closed questions don't offer any explanation of answers, while remote questionnaires may be misinterpreted by users resulting in less reliable data.

👎 Response rate is usually very low.

2 Interview

This is a focused one-to-one meeting with an individual where an interviewer asks questions. This could be face-to-face, over the phone or online using video conferencing.

👍 Follow-up questions can be asked, giving more detailed understanding of answers.

👍 Personal contact can elicit greater honesty from the respondent.

👎 It takes a significant amount of time to gather data from a range of people.

👎 Data is less quantitative than from questionnaires and so harder to analyse.

3 Focus group

This type of survey involves a group of people who are invited to take part. The participants answer questions and share ideas by engaging in conversation.

👍 It is quicker to gather information from a large group than from individuals.

👍 Respondents react to each other's answers, providing very detailed data.

👎 Assembling a group of people at the same time can be difficult.

👎 As with interviews, the qualitative data can be hard to analyse.

Now try this

Choose two sources from questionnaire, interview or focus group. Make sure you look at both the advantages and the disadvantages of each.

> Haldtech Ltd is developing a new product in order to enter the mobile computing market. It needs to find out what its potential customers are looking for.

Analyse two primary sources of collecting data that Haldtech Ltd could use in order to find this out.

Processing data

Data is invaluable to organisations and individuals. It is used to make decisions, spot trends, gain competitive advantage and to monitor progress. It is at the heart of a modern company.

Importance of data accuracy

Inaccurate data can be a serious problem for organisations and individuals, as it leads to incorrect decisions being made. For example:

- incorrectly recorded stock levels could lead to ordering too little or too much stock
- inaccurate traffic information could lead to being late for an interview.

Methods of ensuring data accuracy

IT systems allow us to apply automated checks on data being entered. These do not ensure the data is 100 per cent accurate, but they do ensure it is sensible and matches the original source.

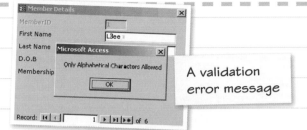

A validation error message

Method	Checks carried out	Examples
Validation ensures data entered is sensible and reasonable.	Type check – data must be the correct type.	Date in a date of birth field.
	Range check – numerical data must be between set values.	Age must be between 18 and 65.
	Length check – data must be less than or greater than a certain number of digits.	First name must be less than 15 characters.
	Format check – data must be in the correct predefined format.	Postcode must be LLN NLL.
Verification ensures data entered matches the original source.	Double entry check – data must be entered twice, and both entries must match.	Entering a password twice on a registration form.
	Proofreading check – data must be read through to ensure there are no data entry errors.	A checkbox asking you to confirm data entered is correct.

Extracting and sorting data

1 Data is extracted from unstructured sources, such as web pages (web scraping), emails and documents.

2 The data is entered into a system for processing.

3 The data is stored in a database program to add structure.

4 The database can be sorted and searched using SQL queries.

Numerical and data modelling

- **Data modelling** ensures that the database is correctly structured, allowing the data to be efficiently processed.
- Correctly stored data can be used in **numerical modelling**. This involves simulating systems to help analyse data and make predictions, such as weather models used to forecast future weather patterns.

Now try this

A new social media site has a registration page that allows users to sign up to use its services.

Make sure your examples are relevant to the sort of data entered into a website registration form.

Describe two validation methods and one verification method that could ensure data is correctly entered into the form.

Data presentation and trend analysis

Data that is presented effectively can be interpreted easily and used to identify trends. Poorly presented data can waste time and not provide the information needed.

Data presentation

Data is meaningless unless it is presented in a way which allows decision makers to use it to inform their decisions. There are many tools available to present data.

	A	B	C	D	E	F
1	Quote Date	Quote No	First Name	Surname	Total Cost	Source
2	09/05/2016	1	Angela	Birkenshaw	£ 350.00	Advertisement
3	13/05/2016	2	Amy	Farmer	£ 459.00	Other
4	28/05/2016	3	Simon	Richards	£ 1,366.40	Advertisement
5	04/06/2016	4	Mitesh	Khan	£ 1,058.40	Advertisement
6	11/06/2016	5	Albert	Tattersall	£ 1,117.60	Advertisement
7	15/06/2016	6	Stephen	Hetherington	£ 642.06	Advertisement
8	16/06/2016	7	Imran	Patel	£ 950.00	Advertisement
9	21/06/2016	8	Ali	Zafar	£ 459.00	Other
10	23/06/2016	9	Jordan	Bamber	£ 1,117.60	Advertisement

Data presented as text is not particularly easy to digest but it does offer some advantages: it is straightforward to find the detail of the thing you are analysing without having to interpret pictorial representations.

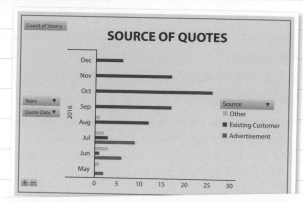

Charts allow you to immediately get a 'feel' for the data. Extremes can be seen at a glance and businesses can identify trends.

There are a wide range of charts available including line, bar, pie, scatter, radar and surface.

Trend analysis

Businesses that can identify trends quickly and easily are the ones which stay ahead of the competition. The more data available, the more accurate and valid the trends should be.

	A	B
1	Date	Sales Amount
2	06/06/2015	5,950.00
3	05/06/2015	6,800.00
4	15/06/2015	6,885.00
5	04/07/2015	6,885.00
6	29/06/2015	7,225.00
7	01/08/2015	7,290.00
8	20/08/2015	7,290.00
9	24/09/2015	7,290.00
10	19/10/2015	7,290.00
11	03/06/2015	7,650.00
12	07/06/2015	7,650.00
13	15/08/2015	7,650.00
14	16/06/2015	7,820.00
15	22/06/2015	7,820.00

A large dataset is meaningless at first glance. A company owner would spend a long time searching through to identify trends by looking at figures alone.

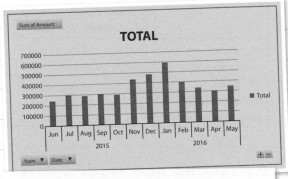

However, by changing the data and performing some grouping, and presenting it in a graphical form, you can see that sales peak during the winter months.

This analysis of trend data allows an organisation to plan things like staffing and stock. More detailed data allows for more detailed predictions. It may be that sales of certain products peak at certain times of year.

A 'pivot chart' could combine sales data and cross reference sales per month with individual product lines to identify which lines perform well or not at different times of year. Pivot charts are excellent at combining massive data sets to compare two (or more) variables.

Now try this

Frank owns a small café in the city centre and often needs to take staff on at short notice to meet demand.

Describe how Frank might use the data he already has about sales to forward plan his staffing levels.

Think about what tools Frank could use and how he might present data in different ways to help him forecast his business's trading patterns.

Presenting data and results

User interfaces of database systems are used to collect data for processing and to output the results to users, so that they can interpret and use that data. How effectively the data is presented affects how useful it is to an organisation.

Presenting data and results

Relational database applications and spreadsheets are used to present information in a variety of formats. This could include:

Tabular data – tables can be formatted, sorted and searched to produce outputs.

Graphical data – a variety of formatted charts to present information in an easy to interpret format.

Error reduction

A good user interface helps to reduce errors when data is inputted, for example by:

- automating certain aspects, for example by providing dropdown list boxes, spinners and checkboxes to enable data entry without typing
- labelling input areas so users know what to enter in each box
- providing warnings when incorrect data is entered
- using techniques such as colour to indicate data entry.

Ease of use and accessibility

A user interface needs to make it easy for users to navigate, input data and receive outputs, regardless of disability, such as limited motor function or visual impairment.

Intuitiveness

An intuitive user interface allows users to easily work out how to use both the interface and the data it provides without a lot of training.

Clear navigation, good labelling and choosing the right output formats all help to improve intuitiveness.

Functionality

The user interface must allow an organisation to make use of the data stored in the ways that it requires. For example, the organisation may wish to carry out certain types of calculation or produce specific types of report. For instance, a report detailing items that are out of stock, rather than just a full stock report, allows for more efficient working.

Performance and compatibility

A system needs to be able process the inputs to the user interface and present outputs quickly. Poor performance leads to frustration and reduces productivity.

The system needs to be compatible with other systems that either input data into the system or receive outputs from it.

Now try this

A business needs to store data from a customer satisfaction survey it performed in order to process and present the results.

Give explanations that are relevant to the type of data that might be collected from a customer satisfaction survey.

Explain two characteristics of a user interface that will help make it easier for the business to input the data.

Moral and ethical issues 1

The use of IT systems has changed how we live our lives and do business, with both positive and negative effects. As a result there are different moral and ethical issues which both producers and users of IT systems need to consider.

Environment

- The ever-growing demand for electronic devices means increased manufacturing output and increased energy needed to run the devices.
- These have negative by-products such as greenhouse gases which affect climate change.

Our constant need to update IT systems has led to increasing amounts of 'technotrash' in landfills.

Unequal access

Not everyone has access to IT systems and the internet.

- There is a distinct divide between access in countries in the developing and developed world.
- Many schools and colleges make resources available online. Students who do not have computer access at home may be disadvantaged in their learning.

Online behaviour

Netiquette describes acceptable behaviour on the internet. It attempts to solve problems such as:

- the perception of the internet as an impersonal and anonymous place to communicate, leading to unacceptable behaviour online
- trolling and cyberbullying on social networking sites, which also affect people's offline lives.

Globalisation

Globalisation describes the process of countries becoming increasingly interconnected, particularly the increase in trade, transport and communications.

- IT systems have played a key role in facilitating this process.
- Despite obvious benefits, globalisation has also caused or exacerbated problems such as job outsourcing, disease spreading, environmental damage and terrorism.

Freedom of speech

Some users of sites, such as social networking, blogs, vlogs and forums, express views that many people find offensive.

- Many sites set rules for the content added by users and for user behaviour, and close down accounts, groups and pages that are in breach of these rules.
- Some users feel this is a form of censorship and a violation of their freedom of speech.

Acceptable use

Many companies have acceptable use policies that define how employees can use IT systems, such as websites and email while at work.

Employees who use IT systems for activities not allowed under acceptable use policies can be subject to disciplinary action.

Now try this

Explain two moral and ethical issues faced by people who use IT systems in order to express their views online.

Look at the issues identified on this page and choose the two that are most relevant to this particular use of IT systems.

Moral and ethical issues 2

Many of the issues that arise from the use of IT systems are covered by legislation (see pages 38 and 39) but there are also moral and ethical concerns associated with these issues.

Health and safety

Health and safety issues associated with IT systems include the risk of repetitive strain injury (RSI), eye and back problems.

Employers have a moral responsibility to carry out risk assessments and provide suitable equipment and working conditions for employees.

Providing ergonomic workstations is part of an employer's duty to its employees.

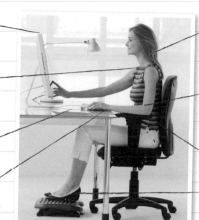

- Top of monitor to be at or just below eye level
- Relaxed shoulders
- Enough space for keyboard and mouse
- Wrists and hands are in line with forearms
- Balanced head and neck, in line with body
- Elbows are supported and close to body
- Lower back is supported
- Feet flat on floor

Copyright

Illegally downloading movies, TV shows, music and software has become more prevalent with the growth of IT systems and services such as bit torrents and online streaming. Likewise the availability of images on the internet increases the risk of people infringing copyright in their work.

These practices threaten the livelihood of the people who produce these works, and those who sell and distribute them.

Protection of data

Organisations and individuals have an ethical responsibility to protect the data of other people that they are using, storing and transmitting.

Computer misuse

Attacks on computer systems, such as viruses, hacking and denial of service (DoS) attacks cause harm to individuals and businesses.

The effects can include loss of income for businesses, loss of jobs, theft of personal wealth, and the upset resulting from the inability to use our IT systems.

Links For more on computer misuse see pages 25, 27 and 38.

Links For more on data protection see pages 27 and 38.

Privacy

Privacy can be compromised by IT systems. Many of us use social networking sites, blogs, online messaging, email and a wide variety of other services to share large parts of our lives online. The growth of services, such as location aware targeted advertising and software, blurs the lines between our online and offline worlds.

The misuse of this information can have severe negative impacts. Cyberbullying, identity theft and bank theft are examples.

Accessibility

New IT systems should be accessible to people regardless of disability.

Inaccessible systems cause upset and stress, and can deny people with disabilities access to work, services and leisure facilities.

Links For more on accessibility see page 39.

Now try this

An online business gathers personal information on its customers when they register for their website. They also record information on customers' buying habits while using the site.

Explain two moral and ethical issues the business needs to consider when gathering this information.

You need to relate each of the issues to the case study given. Copyright, for example, would not be particularly relevant here.

Legislation protecting users and data

You need to know about the role and implications of the main UK legislation for protecting data and users.

Legislation affecting use of IT systems

- Protects the rights of creators of original pieces of work (e.g. music, video, books). This prevents others distributing this work without the copyright holder's permission.

Copyright, Designs and Patents Act 1988

- This covers consumer rights regarding goods and services, including digital content.

- Consumers have the right to repair, replacement or refund for faulty digital content.

Consumer Rights Act 2015

- This act is an amendment to the Computer Misuse Act so that it covers denial of service attacks (DoS). (A DoS aims to disrupt an IT system, e.g. a web server, and prevent user access.)

Police and Justice Act 2006 (Computer Misuse)

- Breach of the act incurs penalties of up to 10 years imprisonment and unlimited fines.

Data Protection Act 1998

Legislation

- The maximum sentence for a DoS attack is 10 years in prison.

Computer Misuse Act 1990

The Health and Safety (Display Equipment) Regulations 1992

The Copyright (Computer Programs) Regulations 1992

- These regulations require organisations to make sure that display equipment, e.g. computer monitors, meet health and safety standards.

- Failure to meet the regulations is punishable by up to two years imprisonment and unlimited fines.

- It makes company board directors liable to prosecution for allowing illegally copied software to be used in their organisation.

- This extends the Copyright, Designs and Patents Act to include computer programs.

Links The Data Protection Act and Computer Misuse Act are covered on page 27.

Why legislate?
- Legislation ensures compliance.
- It encourages and builds trust in systems.
- Ubiquitous computing means our virtual lives are as important to us as our real lives.

Who benefits?
- Individuals – they can trust systems and be sure their personal data is protected.
- Society – the use of powers is transparent and clear.
- Organisations – their reputation is ensured.

Now try this

Simon likes to copy his favourite music from the CD to his computer hard drive so he can listen to it all without needing the discs. He has recently started to upload his music to his own website so others can download and listen to it.

Explain which legislation Simon is breaking and the implications he will face as a result.

 Make sure you name the law, describe it and explain the punishment Simon could receive.

Legislation ensuring accessibility

Legislation in IT is not just about protecting users and data. It is also there to ensure that businesses make their systems accessible to all users and that users with disabilities do not suffer from discrimination.

Accessibility legislation and codes of practice

Legislation	Role	Relevance to IT systems
Disability Discrimination Acts 1995 and 2005 Equality Act 2010	Until 2010 the Disability and Discrimination Act was the main legislation banning discrimination on the basis of disability. When it was passed in 2010, the Equality Act brought together and replaced a number of laws, including the Disability Discrimination Act, creating a single legal framework to ensure equality for all. The act applies to both personal life and the workplace.	Under the Equality Act of 2010, website owners and hosts have obligations to make their sites accessible to all. Service providers must provide special computer software or additional staff support to make their systems accessible, at no extra charge.

Guidelines	Role	Relevance to IT systems
British Standards Institute (BSI) codes of practice	The BSI codes of practice cover a wide range of subjects, including accessibility. They are in place to ensure compliance with legislation.	BSI Standard BS 8878 aims to ensure that web products (e.g. websites, web services and email) are accessible to users with a physical impairment or learning difficulty.
Open Accessibility Framework (OAF)	This European research project sets out a process for ensuring that IT systems are accessible. The framework is broken into steps in two categories: creation of systems, and use of systems.	'Create' steps: 1 Define what accessible means for the particular platform. 2 Provide user interface elements. 3 Provide authoring tools. 'Use' steps: 1 Provide platform supports. 2 Provide accessible software. 3 Provide assistive technologies.
Web Content Accessibility Guidelines (WCAG) 1.0 and 2.0	These guidelines are defined by the World Wide Web Consortium (W3C®) to ensure web content is accessible to all regardless of disability.	The guidelines define three different priority levels for accessibility. Priority level 1 is considered the minimum to allow users with a disability to access a website.

Accessibility and equality

Accessibility isn't about promoting access or giving advantage; it ensures equal access to all, regardless of any impairment or condition. IT and computing offer a great deal by way of assistive technology as far as equality is concerned; so it is essential that this is mirrored within industry.

Now try this

Analyse the impact of legislation and codes of practice on users of IT systems with disabilities.

You need to not just name and describe these, but also look at how they will affect these disabled users.

Your Unit 1 exam

You will have two hours to complete the Unit 1 exam paper. You need to answer **every question**.

Question types

Make sure you look out for the **command** words in exam questions, and that you understand what type of answer is expected for each.

Command words

Assess · Calculate · Complete · Demonstrate · Describe · Discuss · Draw · Explain · Evaluate · Identify · Produce · State/Name/Give · Write · Analyse

Number of marks

In total there will be 90 marks available. Each question will identify the number of marks available in brackets. Questions can be worth up to 12 marks. The number of marks indicate the amount of time you should spend on each question.

1 mark = 1 minute 20 seconds

The amount of writing space available will also give you an idea of how much detail is needed in each of your answers. However, you will be able to request extra paper if you need it.

Practising for the exam

Using practice questions is a great way to revise. You can use the questions in this book, the Revision Workbook and the sample materials provided by the Awarding Body to really get used to the types of questions you'll be asked.

Worked example

Jonathan is an IT security analyst working for a large e-commerce business. It is his job to ensure that the company adheres to the correct legislation and codes of practice.

Explain the role of **two** pieces of legislation in keeping users' data secure.   4 marks

This question is only worth four marks. You should spend about five minutes on your answer.

As this is an 'explain' question you need to do more than just name the relevant legislation – make two clear, distinct points for each piece of legislation.

The question also asks you what 'role' the legislation plays – so you need to explain the consequences of it briefly.

Sample response extract

The Computer Misuse Act makes it illegal for people to gain unauthorised access to IT systems and data by making such activities punishable by jail time and a fine.

The Data Protection Act makes it a legal requirement for businesses to keep users' data secure, accurate and up to date. It punishes businesses that don't comply with massive fines.

You could also mention examples of unauthorised access, such as hacking and spreading malware.

You could also say that a business must only use personal data for clearly specified purposes, or that it must make an individual customer's data available to that customer if they request this.

🔗 **Links** There is more on the Computer Misuse Act and the Data Protection Act on page 27.

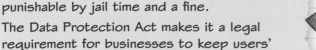
Make sure your factors are relevant to the **workplace**.

Now try this

State **two** different factors that must be considered when choosing IT systems for the workplace.

🔗 **Links** Look at page 14 to revise IT systems in the workplace.

Using case studies

All the exam questions will be based on case studies about a business's or individual's use of IT systems. Each case study will give you all the background information you need to answer the questions effectively. Always read the case study carefully as your answers must relate to it.

Why case studies are important

The case studies allow you to **apply** your knowledge of the unit's content to real-world situations and contexts. This will help you when you move into the working world.

Areas of knowledge you will need to apply

The devices in IT systems
- how devices are used
- the relationships between them

Transmitting data
- connection types
- networks
- the implications

Online IT systems
- online systems and communities
- implications for individuals
- implications for organisations

Protecting data
- implications of storing
- implications of transmitting

Impact of IT systems
- on individuals
- on organisations

Issues involved in using IT systems
- moral and ethical issues
- legislation and codes of practice

Worked example

Each case study will be in a box above the questions, like this

Thomas is a printer repair technician who <u>travels to offices spread all over</u> London to repair printers.

In order to perform his job <u>he uses a tablet to check his work email for new jobs and to report any updates to his managers.</u>

Describe the role of protocols in allowing Thomas to access his emails.   **6 marks**

Sample response extract

There are three main protocols used in email systems. SMTP is used to send Thomas's emails from his email client to his outgoing mail server. It also transfers the email between email servers over the internet.

POP3 is a protocol for retrieving emails from Thomas's incoming mail server. It will download the emails from the server to his device so he can read them offline.

IMAP is an alternative to POP3 where the emails are synced between the server and device rather than downloaded, so Thomas would also be able to access the emails on a different device.

Highlight relevant information

It's a good idea to highlight or underline case study details, as the student has done here, to help you give a specific response to the question.

Here, you could underline the information that Thomas needs to both send and retrieve emails and the device he is using while on the move.

Relate each part of your answer to the case study about Thomas.

This is an 'explain' question, so applying your knowledge of protocols is quite straightforward. An 'evaluate' question might ask you to look at which protocol out of IMAP and POP3 meets Thomas's needs better, so you would need to make sure you fully understand his situation.

Now try this

Olivia is a marketing consultant who has several large organisations as her clients. She has recently started to store all of her clients' information online using cloud storage.

Explain the moral and ethical issues involved in Olivia storing her clients' information on the cloud.

You can gain a lot of information from case studies to help you answer the exam questions. Which key facts would you underline in this question?

 Links Look at pages 36–37 to revise moral and ethical issues, and pages 21–22 to revise cloud computing.

41

Long-answer questions

Up to half the marks in the Unit 1 exam can be assigned to long answer questions (worth 10–12 marks).

Worked example

Harigotts is an investment company that makes heavy use of IT systems to store data and communicate with customers about their investments and finances.

Analyse the threats to the business when using IT systems in this way.

10 marks

This is a 10-mark question so you need to cover a good range of possible threats to IT systems. The command word 'analyse' tells you that you need to show detailed understanding of each threat and set out your answer using a clear structure.

Sample response extract

Malware such as viruses and worms would be a major threat to the data stored by Harrigotts. If a virus infected their systems it could delete the stored data and Harrigotts would lose all the information on their customers' investments. This could lead to losing their customers' investments and would almost certainly result in a loss of business, as customers would be concerned about continuing to invest with Harrigotts.

Another threat could be hackers gaining unauthorised access to Harrigotts' IT systems and modifying or stealing the data being stored. As the company is storing financial information for its customers, this could have severe repercussions, with customers having money stolen from them.

Phishing emails may also be a concern. If Harrigotts are emailing customers regularly, then someone else could send an email to the customers pretending to be Harrigotts. Customers could be tricked into revealing personal information which could be used for identity fraud, such as signing up for loans under a customer's name.

Long answer checklist

A good answer to a 10–12 mark question should:
- ✔ demonstrate **accurate** and **thorough** knowledge
- ✔ apply knowledge to the **context** of the question
- ✔ be well structured and balanced, showing **competing viewpoints**
- ✔ use **technical language** accurately
- ✔ finish with a **supported conclusion** for 'evaluate' questions.

Always relate the threats you have identified to the business in the case study.

Ask yourself, 'How will each threat impact on this particular business?'

Harrigotts may be particularly susceptible to threats because of the financial nature of its business.

Another threat you could mention is accidental damage to the firm's IT systems.

To improve the quality of the response, you could go on to describe aspects of threats such as physical threats, break-ins and/or natural disasters. There might also be internal problems such as employees selling data or using data for another purpose.

Links To revise threats to data, see page 25.

You could structure your answer by examining in turn each of the types of online community the firm is considering.

Now try this

A design firm wants to improve its reputation and increase awareness of the business through the use of online communities. It is considering making use of social networking and blogs for sharing news and interacting with customers, as well as forums for providing customer support.

Evaluate the implications for the firm of using online communities (for practice purposes, you can just plan your answer using bullets).

 Links To revise online communities see pages 23–24.

Remember to focus on the firm's requirements: what are the implications of online communities for interacting with customers and providing customer support?

If time is tight, you could list positive and negative implications and then write a concluding summary paragraph.

This is an 'evaluate' question, so make sure you finish with a conclusion or recommendation for the firm.

Short-answer questions

Short answer questions, with command words such as **identify**, **name**, **state** or **give** want you to give factual information. Answers normally only require a single word or short sentences.

Answering short-answer questions

- Read the question carefully.
- Highlight or underline the key words.
- Look at the number of marks available for the question and make the same number of points (e.g. 2 marks = 2 statements).

- Write the answers in the space provided.
- Provide enough detail but keep to the point.
- If you have enough time once you've completed the exam, re-read your answers to check they make sense and answer the question.

Worked example

Sally runs a wedding photography business. She is considering expanding into new areas of photography and wants to ask customers what photography services they would most like to see.

Name **three** primary methods of gathering information that Sally could use in order to find this out.   **3 marks**

This is a 'name' question, so the examiner isn't looking for detailed explanation, just for the names of different methods of gathering data.

For this question there are three marks, so make sure you identify three primary methods of gathering information.

Sample response extract

To gain feedback from customers on the new services she should provide, Sally could use a questionnaire, focus groups or interviews.

The student has clearly identified three methods of gathering primary data.

Worked example

Danek is setting up a home network that will allow him to wirelessly connect his printer to his computer.

State the two types of network that Danek could use.   **2 marks**

This question is simply asking you to name the appropriate network types. Don't worry about the pros and cons.

Links To revise types of network see page 17.

Sample response extract

Danek could set up a personal area network to connect his laptop to his printer wirelessly. Alternatively he could use a local area network.

Now try this

Adeel has been hired as a graphic designer and his manager has asked him what input devices he will need to complete his work.

Give **three** input devices that Adeel will need.

Links To revise input devices see page 1.

'Draw' questions

If a question asks you to **draw** something, you need to demonstrate your understanding by producing a diagram or a flowchart.

Worked example

A bank uses a registration form in order to allow its customers to sign up for its online banking services. The registration form asks for the following information.

Field name	Field length	Data type
Account number	8	Number
First name	25	Text
Last name	25	Text
Date of birth	N/A	Date/Time
Email	64	Text
Password	12	Text

 Make sure your drawing includes all the data entry fields shown in the table.

Draw a suitable user interface for the bank registration form. **6 marks**

Your user interface could also include:
- instructions for the user on how to complete the form
- appropriate methods to help the user enter their details, such as date picker/calendar for DOB, input mask for password, etc.
- an accessibility feature, such as the 'Listen to this page' feature
- a submit button.

Sample response extract

My Bank plc

Online banking registration form

Please enter your existing account number | *This can be found on your latest bank statement*

Please enter your name Forename *e.g. John*
Surname *e.g. Smith*

Please enter your date of birth dd/mm/yyyy

Please enter your email address example@mybank.com

Please enter a new password

Please re-enter a new password

Passwords must be between 6 and 12 characters long with a mix of letters and numbers

Validation – 8 characters long, just numbers

Validation – Max 25 characters long

Use date selector – Must be in the past

Validate – Must be of the format <something>@<something>.<something>

Validate – At least 6 characters and less than 12

Validate – equal to first password field

Try to make good use of layout and screen space, and make sure your data entry fields are sized appropriately for their purpose.

You can add annotations to explain features of your drawing.

Links To revise user interfaces, see pages 9 and 35.

Make sure you:
- identify all the components mentioned in the question
- identify the additional components needed to form a local area network
- draw the components in the right order with lines connecting them.

Now try this

A business has three computers in its head office which are networked to share documents and to access a single printer.

Draw a diagram of the company's network, identifying all of the devices in the system.

Links To revise different types of network connections, see pages 15 and 16.

'Explain' questions

Questions that ask you to **explain** want you to show that you understand the subject and can give reasons to support a view or argument.

Worked example

WireTech Ltd has decided to improve its sales by making use of online communities to share news and information with its customers.

Explain **two** benefits to WireTech Ltd of using online communities to share news and information with their customers.   **4 marks**

 This question requires you to name the methods of communication using online communities, as well as **explain** how they can be used by WireTech Ltd.

Sample response extract

Wiretech Ltd would benefit as their customers would be able to access help and advice online, and they would be able to promote their products online.

 This learner has briefly described two different benefits of using communities. However, they have not explained how the benefits would be realised and affect WireTech Ltd.

Improved response extract

WireTech Ltd could make use of social media to build up a following of previous customers, therefore being able to respond to their queries. This would benefit WireTech by being able to be more easily aware of their customers' needs and being more acessible to their customer base. WireTech might also provide a blog, or podcasts where they keep customers and potential customers up to date with the company and its products, allowing customers to develop an affinity with the company and potentially boost future sales.

 This is a much better answer. The learner has clearly explained how each method identified could be used by WireTech Ltd and what benefit it brings.

 Links To revise online communities, see pages 23 and 24.

Now try this

Louise needs to send photo images to her family. She can only do so by email but is unsure which image format is the best to use.

Explain the features of **two** different image file formats that would make them appropriate for Louise to use for this task.

 You need to be confident that you can clearly explain why the features of the two file formats you select make them appropriate for photos to be transmitted as email attachments.

 Don't get side-tracked and discuss other methods of sharing photos! Always make sure you answer the question given.

 Links To revise file types, see page 11.

'Analyse' questions

Questions that ask you to **analyse** a topic want you to look into the topic in detail. Break the topic down into its parts and look at the relationship between the parts. This might involve discussing the advantages and disadvantages of possible issues or solutions, but you won't usually be expected to give a conclusion.

Worked example

Hank runs an online business, selling camping and survival equipment. On his website customers are able to purchase products, but first they must register an account using their personal and bank information.

Analyse the impact of **two** different relevant laws on Hank's business.

 6 marks

'Analyse' questions require you to carefully consider the case study. You need to clearly explain the points you are making and always link them to the case study.

For this question you need to:
- identify two laws that are clearly applicable to the case study
- explain each law and show how it will impact on the business.

Sample response extract

There are a number of laws that affect Hank's business. The Data Protection Act, for example, requires Hank to ensure that the personal information he is storing on customers is kept secure. This will affect Hank as he will need to implement a number of security techniques and procedures that could potentially be costly and time consuming.

Another law that Hank is affected by is the Computer Misuse Act. This law makes it illegal for people to gain unauthorised access to Hank's website. This will help Hank's business as it will deter potentially malicious users from hacking his site and stealing, deleting or modifying the personal and bank information that he is storing on customers.

You could also mention other aspects of the Data Protection Act that will affect Hank's business. For example, the need to clearly specify the purposes for which the business is collecting data and to make sure that the data is only used for these purposes. Any misuse of customers' data would make Hank's business liable to pay compensation.

 Links To revise legislation affecting IT systems, see pages 27, 38 and 39.

Now try this

Donna has found recently that the performance of her PC has significantly reduced, especially during the startup process of the PC.

Analyse the role of utility software programs in improving Donna's PC performance (for practice purposes, you can just plan your answer using bullets).

In a full answer, you need to discuss utility programs. You would also need to fully explain what role each program will have in improving Donna's startup performance.

 Links To revise utility software, see page 10.

'Evaluate' questions

If a question asks you to **evaluate** you need to look at all sides of an argument in order to provide a well-supported judgement on a topic or problem. This normally includes writing a supported conclusion or a recommendation for a solution.

Worked example

> Choudhry Solicitors has used the same computers and desktop productivity software since it was founded several years ago. However, the software is now quite dated and the law firm is considering upgrading to a cloud-based software alternative.

Evaluate the firm's decision to start using cloud computing productivity software.

12 marks

Evaluate questions require you to look at both sides of an argument. In this case this involves looking at the pros and cons of cloud computing productivity software.

Sample response extract

Cloud computing would be helpful to the law firm for a number of reasons. Firstly, cloud computing software doesn't put a high demand on the computer's CPU and RAM as it runs on the host's server not the local computer. This will be very helpful as the law firm is using older computers that might not have a high enough specification to be able to run the latest desktop productivity software.

Another benefit is that cloud computing supports collaborative working. The firm's employees can easily work on the same documents using cloud computing as they can share access to the files easily.

A disadvantage of cloud computing is that if the firm loses its internet connection, or if the servers of the cloud computing provider go down, then the employees will not be able to access the software and perform any of the necessary office computing tasks.

Overall, I believe that the law firm should switch to cloud computing software. The fact that cloud computing software doesn't require a lot of processing power will save the law firm money as they won't need to upgrade their computers. The ability to collaborate between employees will also help make the business more efficient. The issue of not being able to access the software without an internet connection is unlikely to affect the firm much, as long as it ensures a good internet connection.

There are a wide variety of pros and cons to cloud computing.
While it is important to mention a range of these, it's more important that you are able to clearly explain the ones you cover in some detail.

Make sure you relate the pros and cons to the case study of the law firm, as this learner has done.

Make sure you provide a clear conclusion at the end, that is a logical decision based on the points you have already made in your answer.

Your answer could be improved if you referred to software costs, interoperability, security and training.

Links To revise cloud computing, see pages 21–22.

Now try this

Remember, in the exam you need to look at the pros and cons of each method and to make a clear, well-argued conclusion.

> A student is performing research on trends in IT systems and the future of emerging technologies. They are trying to find information on how people are currently using IT in their lives and how IT has changed over the past five years.

Evaluate the use of primary and secondary sources of data in order for the student to carry out this research (for practice purposes, you can just plan your answer using bullets).

Links To revise data gathering methods, see page 32.

Relational database management systems (RDBMS)

An **RDBMS** is a type of database where data is organised in tables which are related in some way.

Types of relational databases

There are two main ways to categorise database software.

 How many people use the software?

- **Desktop** systems (e.g. Microsoft Access) are for individual users.
- **Client-server-based** systems and **web-based** systems (e.g. Microsoft SQL Server and MySQL) are for multiple users.

 Is the software open source or not?

- **Open source** software (e.g. MySQL) is available to use free of charge.
- **Proprietary software** (e.g. Microsoft Access) requires a paid licence.

Functions of database software

The range of functions performed by RDBMS software includes:

- manipulation of data, such as updating, inserting, and deleting records
- retrieval of data for queries and reports
- administration of users, including the data and facilities they can and cannot access
- maintaining the security and integrity of the data
- recovering the data in case of failure.

Characteristics of relational databases

Contacts table → Appointments table

A relational database is made up of two or more tables of data.

Each table has a unique identifier called the **primary key**. The field within each table used as the primary key is important because this is what makes the link to other tables. It is best to use a made-up value like an ID number for a primary key.

Links For more on primary keys, see page 52.

Relational database terms

The terminology can be confusing because different software products use different names. Look at this example of a single table holding data for the contacts in an address book.

- Data is divided up into defined **fields** or **attributes**.
- A **table** is sometimes called a **relation**.

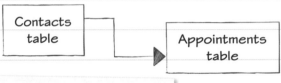

ID_Number	First Name	Last Name	Age	Phone No.
1	Alan	Jones	38	079998888
2	Mohammed	Iqbal	28	077776666
3	Sally	Smith	22	074441111
4				
5				

The number of unique values for a given field is known as its **cardinality**.

Primary key field

Each row of data is called a **record** or **tuple**.

The range of acceptable values for a field is known as its **domain**, so the domain for the age field might be 0–120.

Now try this

Match each database term to the correct definition.

Terms

1 Primary key   2 Tuple (or record)   3 Relation   4 Attribute (or field)   5 Domain   6 Cardinality

Definitions

(a) A table row   (b) Another name for a table   (c) A table column   (d) A unique identifier
(e) The number of records in a table   (f) The range of acceptable values

What are entities?

In software engineering you are often faced with the problem of trying to design complex systems. In database design one concept that is often used to try to model the relationships between the 'things' in the system is **entity relationship modelling**.

What are entities?

Entities are 'things' in the system you are trying to model.

- Entities can be real life things like students, customers, cars, products (like a TV set or a kettle).
- Entities can also be concepts rather than real life objects, for example loans, orders or courses.

In the database design entities become database tables.

How are entities related?

This is the key question!

- During the design stage of database development, understanding how different entities are related helps you understand the system.
- Generally, entities are nouns (for example, 'customer' and 'order'), while the relationship between them is described by a verb (for example 'places').
- For example, a customer **places** an order or a patient **is allocated to** a doctor.
- This basic understanding of how entities are related is known as **generic** modelling.

Entity relationship diagrams

You need to draw an **entity relationship diagram (ERD)** at the design stage of a database development project to show the entities and the relationships between them.

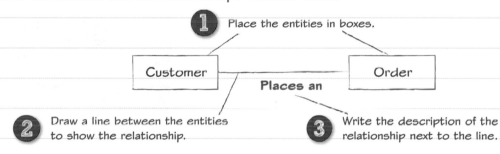

1 Place the entities in boxes.

Customer — Places an — Order

2 Draw a line between the entities to show the relationship.

3 Write the description of the relationship next to the line.

The relationships in a complex system can be quite involved.

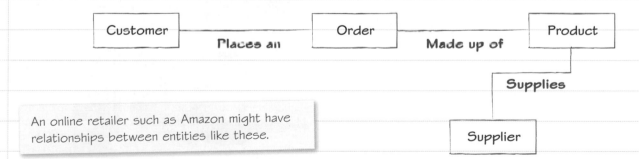

Customer — Places an — Order — Made up of — Product — Supplies — Supplier

An online retailer such as Amazon might have relationships between entities like these.

Now try this

Imagine you are developing a database system for your college or school to record details of students and the different courses they are enrolled on.

1 What would the entities be in this system?
2 How would they be related?

Think about how you might keep records of students, classes, tutors and courses.

49

Entity relationships: one-to-one and one-to-many

Having decided what the entities in a system are, and how they are related (your generic model of the database), the next step is to consider what type of relationship exists between them. You can then develop a more detailed, logical model, sometimes called a **semantic** model.

Types of relationships

There are three types of relationship possible:

1 one-to-many

2 one-to-one

3 many-to-many.

Characteristics

These are the characteristics of the first two relationship types:

- A **one-to-many relationship** is the most common type. This is where one record in an entity is related to many records in another entity.
- A **one to-one relationship** is where one record in an entity is related to only one record in another entity.

Drawing a one-to-many relationship

Each individual patient is only allocated to one doctor

One doctor is allocated many patients.

```
  Patient >——————————  Doctor
          Allocated to
```

The 'many' end of the relationship is indicated by the 'crow's foot' and/or the infinity symbol.

Take care when drawing ERDs. If you forget to add the 'crow's foot' to a one-to-many relationship, it just looks like a one-to-one relationship.

In a GP surgery the relationship between a doctor and patients is one-to-many (ONE doctor MANY patients).

Drawing a one-to-one relationship

This type of relationship is much less common. Imagine a plumbing business that employs 10 plumbers. Each plumber is allocated a van that they drive to customers. Each plumber can only drive one van.

```
                Drives
  Plumber ——————————————  Van
```

🔗 **Links** Many-to-many relationships are a little more difficult to understand and are covered on page 51.

The relationship between plumbers and vans is one-to-one (ONE plumber ONE van).

Now try this

Imagine a system which records data on football teams and players. What type of relationship would exist between the Teams and Players tables? Can you draw the ERD for this relationship?

Entity relationships: many-to-many

Many-to-many relationships between entities do sometimes occur in database design. This is where many records in one entity can be related to many records in another entity. You need to know how to deal with these.

Dealing with many-to-many relationships

- You cannot represent a direct **many-to-many relationship** in a relational database.
- You need to identify these relationships and resolve them at the design stage.

An example

- If you are designing a database for a school or college, it's likely you will need to include entities for students and subjects.
- In most schools and colleges students study a number of different subjects or units, so one student record will be related to many subjects.
- Also, one subject is studied by lots of students, so one subject record will be related to many students.

This is therefore a many-to-many relationship.

Resolving a many-to-many relationship

You cannot represent the many-to-many relationship shown in the diagram in your database design.

One student takes many subjects.

Student — Many-to-many — Subject

Each subject is taken by many students.

To resolve a many-to-many relationship, you need to create a **link entity** (that is, a table that sits between the two entities).

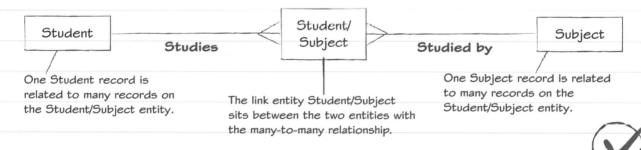

Student — **Studies** — Student/Subject — **Studied by** — Subject

One Student record is related to many records on the Student/Subject entity.

The link entity Student/Subject sits between the two entities with the many-to-many relationship.

One Subject record is related to many records on the Student/Subject entity.

Now try this

A database for an online store might have the following relationships: customers place orders, and orders consist of products. But a single order can have many products on it. This is potentially a many-to-many relationship: a product can appear on many orders and an order can have many products on it.

How can you resolve this?

Relational keys

Once you have drawn the ERD showing the entities and the relationships (including the type of relationships) between them, the next step in understanding how relational databases are designed is to investigate the role that keys (sometimes called **indexes**) have in entity relationships.

The primary key

- Every entity (or table) in a relational database should have a **primary key**.
- The primary key is a unique identifier for a table.
- Every record in a table must have a different (unique) primary key.
- The primary key makes it easier to identify the correct record in a large table.

What makes a good primary key?

Because the primary key values in a table must be unique, using a field such as 'name' or even 'date of birth' is not a good idea. Therefore, primary key values are usually a 'made-up' code such as a customer ID number or an order number.

Types of keys

A primary key is not the only type of key.

Primary key
When creating the relationship between entities, the primary key is used to uniquely identify the record at the 'one' end of a one-to-many relationship.

Foreign key
A copy of the primary key value is taken from the record at the 'one' end and placed in a field in the records at the 'many' end. This is a **foreign key**.

Database keys

Candidate keys
When designing a complex database, you may have a choice of several different fields to use as a primary key. Fields which could be used as the primary key are referred to as **candidate keys**.

Super key
You can create a key by combining two different fields. This is known as a **super key** or **composite key**.

How to use primary and foreign keys

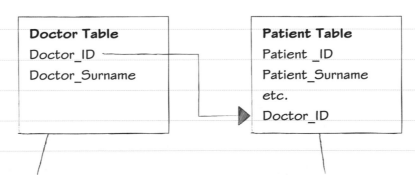

On the Doctor Table the field 'Doctor_ID' is the primary key. It is the unique identifier for each doctor.

On the Patient Table the field 'Doctor_ID' is the foreign key. When a patient is allocated to a doctor, that doctor's primary key field value from the Doctor Table is placed in the foreign key field.

Now try this

In a database for an online store there will be entities (tables) for customers, orders, products and suppliers.
Work out what the primary and foreign keys should be in each of these entities.

Database integrity

One of the most important things you need to do when designing a database is ensure the **integrity** of the data. This means making sure that the data makes sense and that records cannot be 'lost' or accidentally deleted.

Types of database integrity

- **Physical integrity** means ensuring that the data files on the disk where the database is stored are protected, for example by regular backup and using RAID disk systems.

- **Referential integrity** means that there must always be a related record in table with the 'one' part of the relationship. For example an order must have a related customer, as an order cannot exist without a customer.

- **Entity integrity** involves ensuring that records on a table have a primary key that is unique.

Integrity issues

One type of entity integrity problem is a **delete anomaly**.

Customer table

Cust_No	Name	etc.
01234	Smith	xxxx

 1 Records on the customer table are related to the order table using the primary key value in the customer table (Cust_No).

 2 If you delete the record on the Customer table, there will be records on the Order table that have no corresponding customer.

3 Application programs which access the database may be written expecting the foreign key in every Order table record to link back to a record on the Customer table. If this is not the case, then delete anomalies will occur in these applications.

Order table

Order_No	Cust_No	Date
16592	01234	5/1/16
19886	01234	12/2/16
20451	01234	9/3/16

Other anomalies

- An **insert anomaly** can occur if records are inserted at the 'many' end of the relations with no corresponding record at the 'one' end.

- An **update anomaly** can occur if the key field value of a record at the 'one' end is updated (changed) and the corresponding foreign key values of records at the' many' are not updated.

Cascade delete and cascade update

You need to give careful thought to database integrity during your database design.

Microsoft Access provides these options when creating relationships between tables:

- **Cascade delete** – If you delete a record at the 'one' end of a relationship the related records at the 'many' end are automatically deleted.

- **Cascade updates** – If you update (change) the key field value of a record at the 'one' end, then the corresponding foreign key values of records at the 'many' end are automatically updated.

If you don't have these options switched on, you run the risk of creating delete or update anomalies, which break the link between records in a one-to-many relationship.

Now try this

What is the difference between physical integrity and referential integrity? Why are they important?

Relational algebra

Relational algebra is the mathematical theory that lies behind database technology. It is how SQL (structured query language) is able to create queries to extract information from database tables.

What relational algebra operations are there?

There are a number of different operations you can apply to tables. Each operation is represented by a special character. These are the ones you need to be aware of:

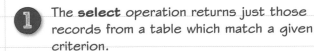

Select
represented by the symbol σ

Intersect
represented by the symbol ∩

Relational algebra operations

Union
represented by the symbol ∪

Join
represented by the symbol ⋈

How do relational algebra operations work?

1 The **select** operation returns just those records from a table which match a given criterion.

For example, if you have a table of cars, with makes, models and specifications and you want to extract all the cars made by Ford, the select operation will be:

σ Make = "Ford"^(Cars)

The field   The criterion   The table name

2 The **union** operation is very simple and involves combining two tables, which have the same fields, together.

Table1 ∪ Table2

This operation will return all the records in Table1 combined with the records in Table2.

3 The **intersect** operation is similar to union except that only those records which appear in **both** tables are selected.

Table1 ∩ Table2

This operation will select only the duplicate records which are on both Table1 and Table2.

Join

4 **Join**, as the name suggests, joins two tables together. The two tables must have at least one common field. For example, imagine you want to join these two tables:

Cars_for_sale

Make	Model	Dealer
Ford	Fiesta	Central Motors
VW	Golf	Bridge Garage
Renault	Clio	Central Motors
Vauxhall	Corsa	Bridge Garage

Dealers

Dealer	Address	Town
Central Motors	High Street	Luton
Bridge Garage	Bridge Street	Watford

The operation   **Cars_for_sale ⋈ Dealers**   will produce:

Make	Model	Dealer	Address	Town
Ford	Fiesta	Central Motors	High Street	Luton
VW	Golf	Bridge Garage	Bridge Street	Watford
Renault	Clio	Central Motors	High Street	Luton
Vauxhall	Corsa	Bridge Garage	Bridge Street	Watford

Now try this

Match each relational algebra operation to its description.

1 Join   (a) combines two tables which have the same fields.
2 Select   (b) combines two tables, selecting just the records which occur in both.
3 Intersect   (c) combines two tables which have at least one common field.
4 Union   (d) selects records from a table based on a given criterion.

Normalisation

Normalisation is a design process which is often used to check the structure of the ERD.

What is normalisation?

ERDs model the system by identifying entities and their relationships.

In contrast, **normalisation** takes the existing data from the system being developed and applies a logical process to divide up the data into tables.

The purpose of normalisation

Unnormalised data is data in its 'raw' form. Depending on the particular system, it might come from paper-based records or other sources.

The key purposes of normalisation are to ensure that there is no **data redundancy** (which means no unnecessary duplication of data) and to make the database as efficient as possible.

How is data normalised?

This is 'raw' unnormalised data kept by a company selling computer games.

1 The first step in normalising data is to look for repeating data. This is where the same data is repeated across many records.

The same consoles are repeated several times.

Stock no.	Game title	Publisher	Release date	Console	Genre	Price
1	Far Cry	UBI Soft	1/10/15	PS4	Adventure	£25.99
2	Minecraft	Telltale	6/3/15	Xbox 360	Adventure	£19.99
3	Need for Speed	EA	5/8/15	PS4	Racing	£34.99
4	F1 2015	Namco	1/4/15	PS4	Racing	£15.99
5	WRC 5	UBI Soft	6/8/15	PS4	Racing	£22.00
6	Plants vs Zombies	EA	1/2/16	Xbox 360	Action	£36.00
7	Another game	Namco	1/1/15	Xbox 360	Action	£22.00

2 Fields with repeating data and any other fields associated with them are moved to another table.

Console_ID	Console name
1	Xbox 360
2	PS 4

A new Console table is used to store a single occurrence of each console type.

A primary key is created for the new Console table. This is used as a foreign key in the original table linking to the new table.

Stock no.	Game title	Publisher	Release date	Console_ID	Genre	Price
1	Far Cry	UBI Soft	1/10/15	1	Adventure	£25.99
2	Minecraft	Telltale	6/3/15	2	Adventure	£19.99
3	Need for Speed	EA	5/8/15	1	Racing	£34.99
4	F1 2015	Namco	1/4/15	1	Racing	£15.99
5	WRC 5	UBI Soft	6/8/15	1	Racing	£22.00
6	Plants vs Zombies	EA	1/2/16	2	Action	£36.00
7	Another game	Namco	1/1/15	2	Action	£22.00

Now try this

1 More information (fields) could be added to the Console table. Can you suggest what these fields might be?

2 There is another group of repeating data, as well as Console, which could be moved to another table. Which field is it in?

The stages of normalisation

The process of normalisation is divided into a number of stages. You need to be able to carry out the first three stages.

What are the stages?

At each stage the original 'unnormalised' data is further modified and refined. The stages are:

- UNF – un-normalised or raw data
- INF – 1st normal form
- 2NF – 2nd normal form
- 3NF – 3rd normal form.

Dependence

The normalisation process involves checking if a field in a table **depends** on another field. To do this, ask the question:

'Can I find the value of the second field if I know the first?'

For example, think of a table of car registration numbers and details (make, model, etc.).

👍 If you know the registration number then you can find the make of the car. So make depends on registration number.

👎 However, if you know the car make you can't find the registration number, as there will be lots of registration numbers associated with the same make. So registration number does not depend on make (or model).

What happens at each stage?

At each stage you need to check the data you have meets the requirements of the stage. If it does not, you will need to modify it so that it does. These are the requirements of each stage.

1 **1st normal form (1NF)**

- Each field must be **atomic**, which means it cannot be broken down any further. For example, you might have a field called Address. You need to break this down into Address line 1, Address line 2, Town, County, Postcode, etc.
- Check for repeating data. If you find any, move it to a separate table.
- Each table should have a unique primary key. If no single field contains unique values, it may be possible to create a primary key by combining more than one field, creating a composite key. Alternatively (and more commonly) you can simply use a 'made up' numeric value as a unique primary key value.

Primary and foreign keys

Remember, when you split a table into two separate tables, you take the primary key from the first table and add it as a field in the new table as the foreign key. The new table will also need a primary key of its own.

2 **2nd normal form (2NF)**

- This stage only applies if any of the tables resulting from the 1NF modifications have a composite key.
- If they do, you need to check if any of the fields in the table are dependent on just one part of the composite key.
- If they are, move them to a separate table.

3 **3rd normal form (3NF)**

- The tables should contain no dependences.
- Check each of the fields in the tables you have at 2nd normal form, apart from the primary key fields.
- Ask yourself, 'Does this field depend on any other field in the table?'
- If you find any fields that do depend on another field, move them to another table.

Now try this

At which normalisation stage (1NF, 2NF or 3NF) do you do the following?

(a) Check the dependences of a composite key.

(b) Make sure data is atomic.

(c) Check the dependences of all the fields except the primary key.

(d) Move repeating data to another table.

Data dictionary

Having confirmed the ERD design using the normalisation process, the next stage in developing the database design is to create the **data dictionary**.

What is a data dictionary?

The data dictionary lists all the fields and their **attributes** for each table you identified in your ERD and during the normalisation process.

Attributes

A data dictionary needs to list the following for every field in a table:

- the **field names**
- the **data type**
- the **field size**
- **validation** (if any) to be applied to the field.

Data dictionary example

This example shows the data dictionary for the Games table in a database for a company that sells computer games.

Table name	Games
Field name	**Attributes**
Stock_ID	Primary key, integer
Game_title	Text, 25 characters, no validation
Publisher	Text, 25 characters, no validation
Release date	Date data type, format dd/mm/yy
Console_ID	Foreign key, must appear on the Console table.
Genre	Text, uses a lookup table with values 'Adventure', 'Racing', 'Action' and 'Role Play'.
Price	Currency data type, must be greater than £0.99 and less than £150.00

Be consistent in your **naming conventions** for field names, for example in your use of capital letters. Use underscores rather than spaces.

Give careful thought to the validation you apply to these kinds of fields, where it may not be obvious what the upper and lower limits should be. You need to be quite sure there is no possibility or will be no need to enter values outside the limits you set.

Where a field has a limited number of possible entries, you can use a **lookup table**. (Another example is a field holding a person's gender where the only valid entries are M or F.)

 Links This database uses the data shown on page 55.

Automatic validation

In Microsoft Access, some data types automatically validate entries. For example, the date data type automatically rejects invalid dates, and a field with a numeric data type will not allow users to enter text values.

Links For more on validation, see pages 67, 68 and 69.

Now try this

As well as a table for games, the database for the computer games company is likely to have a table for consoles. Create a data dictionary for a Consoles table, adding the fields you think it should have and their attributes.

Manipulating data structures and data: SQL – Create and Insert

Structured query language (SQL) is not like a traditional programming language as you don't use it to write long programs. Instead you create commands to manipulate and extract data from a relational database.

SQL Create

The Create command lets you create a table. Here is the syntax of the command:

```
CREATE TABLE table_name
  (
  field_name_1 datatype(size),
  field_name_2 datatype(size),
  ...
  );
```

Data types include:
- Int – for integers
- Decimal – for numbers with a fractional part
- Date – for dates
- Varchar – for text.

Example SQL Create command

This example is used to create a Cars table.

```
CREATE TABLE Cars
(
Car_ID int,
Make varchar(25),
Model varchar(25),
No_of_doors int,
Engine_size int,
MPG float,
Top_speed int
);
```

The int data type does not need a field length.

SQL View in Microsoft Access

Database software like Microsoft Access provides an easy to use interface to create tables, but you can use SQL instead by clicking the View icon on the Home tab and choosing SQL View.

When you have a query open, you can select SQL View from the View menu.

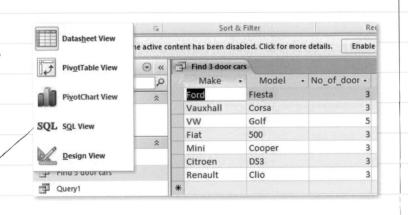

SQL Insert Into

To **insert data** into a table you use the SQL Insert Into command. The syntax of the command is:

```
INSERT INTO table_name
VALUES (value1, value2, value3...);
```

Example SQL Insert Into command

To insert a record into the Cars table created above, the SQL command is:

```
INSERT INTO Cars
VALUES(1, 'Ford', 'Fiesta', 3,
1300, 42, 105);
```

Text values are enclosed in single quotes, numeric values are not.

Now try this

Use SQL commands to create the Cars table and insert a record following the examples on this page. Then add eight to ten more records to the Cars table using the SQL Insert Into command.

Manipulating data structures and data: SQL Select

The SQL Select command is used to retrieve specific records from your database for queries and for use in reports.

SQL Select

If you want to select all the records from a table use this syntax:

```
SELECT * FROM table_name;
```

If you want to select only certain columns from the table use this syntax:

```
SELECT column_name, column_name
FROM table_name;
```

Example SQL Select command

The command in this example selects just the Make, Model and No_of_doors fields from the Cars table.

```
SELECT Make, Model, No_of_doors
FROM Cars;
```

Make	Model	No_of_door
Ford	Fiesta	3
Vauxhall	Corsa	3
BMW	316	4
VW	Golf	5
Fiat	500	3
Toyota	Corolla	6
Mini	Cooper	3
Citroen	DS3	3
*		

The example command will return something like this (depending on the cars data you entered into your table).

SQL Select Where

Select Where is a more powerful version of the Select command. It allows you to select records that meet certain criteria. Suppose you just want to select the cars made by Ford, the command will be:

```
SELECT * FROM Cars WHERE Make =
'Ford';
```

Note that when using a text field in a Select Where command, the criterion must be in quotes.

If you just want to see the three-door cars, the command will be:

```
SELECT * FROM Cars WHERE
No_of_doors = 3;
```

When using a numeric field you don't use quotes.

These two examples use '*' to display all fields, but you can list the fields you want to display as in the example for the SQL Select command above.

Comparison operators

With numeric values you can use comparison operators as well as the equals sign.

> means greater than (so No_of_doors > 2 will find all records with cars that have 3 or more doors).

< means less than.

>= means greater than or equal to.

<= means less than or equal to.

Links You can also use Boolean operators such as AND and OR. These are covered on page 72.

Now try this

Work out what the SQL instructions will be to extract the following data from the Cars table:

(a) Cars made by Ford, showing just the model name and engine size.

(b) All cars with 4 doors, showing the make and model fields only.

(c) All cars with MPG (miles per gallon) higher than 40, showing all fields.

 For question **(c)**, use the greater than symbol '>' rather than '='.

Relational database design steps

Database design is similar to other software development design processes but there are a few aspects which are specific to databases.

How do you design a database?

These are the basic steps you need to follow when designing a database.

Step 1: Understand the user requirements.
- What does the database system need to do?
- What are the entities in the system?
- What are the relationships between them?

You should be able to look at some data from the existing system, whether it is paper based or electronic. This will help you start to identify entities.

Here, you decide the relationships between tables and types of relationship (one-to-many, one-to-one, many-to-many).

Step 2: Perform **entity relationship modelling** and produce ERDs.

These can start off in outline form (**conceptual** models) and be refined later into detailed (**logical**) models.

Step 3: Carry out the normalisation process.

Use the data from the existing system to confirm the ERD you have drawn is correct.

As part of the normalisation process you can decide on the primary key for each table and use it as the foreign key in related tables.

Step 4: Create your data dictionary.

Use the results of the normalisation and the ERD to do this.

Your user interface should allow users to input data and produce outputs in an easy to use format.

Step 5: Design the application.

Create the user interface designs, including data input screens and menus.

Provide menus to allow users to navigate the various features of the system.

Some systems may also require the development of software applications to access the database.

Step 6: Create query and report designs.

Include Boolean operators (AND, OR, NOT) and comparison operators (>, <, ≥, ≤).

You will need to design reports for paper-based outputs. Reports often rely on a query to extract the required data. The output from queries can also be display as a form.

Step 7: Create test plans for tables, forms, queries and reports.

Now try this

(a) Place these design steps in the order you need to complete them:

Create test plans, Normalisation, Understand user requirements, Application design, Create ERDs, Design queries and report, Create data dictionary.

(b) Write a sentence explaining what each step involves.

Relational database design considerations

There are a number of design considerations you need to think about and decide on before you start work on the implementation of your database.

Design considerations

1 **What does the user want?** The user requirements are often defined in a specification which describes the purpose of the system, the audience (users) and the requirements of the client (the person who is paying for the development).

2 **What database system (RDBMS and SQL) will you use?** This may be determined by the type of system you are developing.

- A simple desktop database for a single user can be developed in Microsoft Access.
- Larger multi-user and web-based database systems need to use more sophisticated software such as MySQL or Oracle Database.

3 **Consider the physical modelling of the database.** This includes the hardware that will be used to implement the database and the amount of disk space required.

Database development for real users

The user requirements are key to your database design. While you are learning about database and software development, you will be developing systems to practise your skills. In reality, software products are developed for other people to use, so the developer has to try and 'get in the mind' of the users of the system.

The users of the system and the people paying for it are often different, so the developer has to satisfy both.

Data protection

Many database systems hold personal information, such as people's names and addresses, and therefore come under the Data Protection Act 1998 (and the related EU Data Protection legislation).

Your design needs to ensure that the database meets the requirements of this legislation, including measures to secure the database so that only those users who have a reason to access personal data can do so.

4 **How will you implement the database system?** If the system is replacing an existing one, how will you convert the existing data to the new system? This can be a complex process and may involve reorganising large amounts of data into different tables.

5 **Will you create a prototype?** This is a partial version of the system which allows users to see how the database will look and how its major functions will work. User feedback is then used to refine the prototype and develop the final fully working version.

6 **How will you maintain data integrity?** Your design needs to consider the integrity of the database and how to deal with update, insert and delete anomalies.

Why is design important?

When creating any complex system the design is vital. Unless the design is correct it is very unlikely that the final outcome will be fit for purpose. A good design ensures that the final product is:

- of good **quality** – not full of errors and does not fail frequently
- **effective** at what it does – easy to use and not unduly complex
- **appropriate** – it carries out the functions that were originally defined for it.

🔗 **Links** To revise database integrity, see page 53.

🔗 **Links** For more on the Data Protection Act, see Unit 1, page 27.

Now try this

Write a brief definition for each of these terms related to database design considerations:

(a) physical modelling, (b) prototype, (c) data protection, (d) data conversion.

Design documentation: user interface design

Once you have designed the structure of your database, you need to consider how the user will interact with the database. You will decide what menus and other forms are needed to allow the user to access the facilities of the database and input data.

Types of user interface

Three main types of form are used in user interfaces.

1 **Menu** – your system will need a menu to allow the user to select the different functions that are available.

2 **Data entry forms** – these allow the user to input data to the database. Where possible, include input validation with appropriate error messages.

3 **Data viewing form** – these show individual records from the database. They are sometimes used to display the output from a query.

Your user interface needs to make it easy for users to access and input data.

Designing forms

One of the criteria used to judge your designs is whether they would allow someone else to be able to implement them. Therefore, your interface designs must be detailed and clear, and include:

- a sketch of how the form will look
- information for the user to understand how to use the form (such as labels stating the purpose of each field and providing other hints)
- the database fields to be included on the form, along with any **validation** to be done or input masks to be used
- any calculated fields that may be required, such as an order total which adds up the prices of all the items on an order.

An example form design

This data entry form is for a table in a BTEC database containing BTEC units.

Sketch of the form

Add a BTEC Unit	
Unit Name	*Unit_name*
Unit Number	*Unit_number*
Unit Type	*Unit_type*
GLH	*GLH*
Cancel	Save

Database fields included:

All fields are from the Unit table:

- Unit_name – text, no validation
- Unit_number – integer, must be between 1 and 25
- Unit_type – list box selection from only Internal or External
- GLH – list box selection from only 60, 90 and 120

Now try this

The BTEC database also has a Student table with these fields: ID_number, First_name, Surname, Date_of_birth, Course, Phone_number, Home_address, Town, Postcode.

Design a data input form for this table.
Write a brief definition for each of these terms related to database design considerations: physical modelling, prototype, data protection, data conversion.

If you are using MS Access and the primary key field is an autonumber field, you should not include it on a data entry form. Access will add the value automatically to the field.

Design documentation: reports and task automation

Reports are used when a printed output is needed, such as an order confirmation, a ticket or a financial summary such as an invoice or statement.

Designing reports

There are a couple of things which you need to consider when designing a report:

- Reports are often based on queries which extract the data to be displayed on the report, and so you will design the report and the query together.
- Presentation of a report can be important, especially if the printed report will be given to a customer, as the quality of the report reflects on the organisation.

Report layouts

When designing a report, produce an annotated sketch of the layout to define how it will look and where the data comes from. Here is an example of a design for an order summary report.

Order Number:	nnnnnnn
Order Date:	dd/mm/yy
Customer Number:	nnnnnnn

This data comes from the Order table: Order_no, Order_date and Cust_no).

Item	Description	Unit Price	Quantity	Total
N	xxxxxxxxxxxxxx	£nnn.nn	nn	£nnn.nn
N	xxxxxxxxxxxxxx	£nnn.nn	nn	£nnn.nn
N	xxxxxxxxxxxxxx	£nnn.nn	nn	£nnn.nn
			Grand total:	£nnn.nn

Calculated field: Unit_price * Quantity

Calculated field: sum (total)

This data comes from the Order_line table (Description, Quantity) and is repeated for as many items as are on the order.

Unit price comes from the Products table.

This report is based on a query (Find_order) which selects an individual order from the Order table and combines it with data from the Order_line and Products tables to bring together all the data for the order.

 Links To revise query design see page 64.

Task automation

The user interface does not normally just consist of a collection of forms, queries and reports.

To create an easy to use interface you will probably need to automate some tasks using macros or VBA program code to make things like **importing**, **updating** and **deleting** data easier.

For example, you may not want users to directly delete records. Instead records which are no longer active should be copied to an archive table. Therefore, a 'Delete' button you add to a form may run a macro which copies the record to the archive table before deleting it.

Now try this

Sketch a report design for a database of music concert bookings which prints a customer ticket.

Design documentation: query design

Queries are used to **extract data** from the database. The results of a query can be **presented** using a list format, a form or a report.

What can a query do?

A query can:

- ☑ find data which matches a certain **criterion** or **multiple criteria**:
  - numeric data – find values that are equal to, greater than or less than a given value
  - text data – find values that are equal to or contain part of a text string you provide
- ☑ **sort** data into ascending or descending order based on any field
- ☑ **combine** data from linked records on different tables
- ☑ **calculate** values based on other fields, for example add together two or more fields to create a total (see page 72)
- ☑ pick up data entered on a form, so the criteria for a query can be input using a form
- ☑ carry out more advanced queries (MS Access calls them **Action Queries**) with matching records, such as delete them, add them to a new table or modify them in some way.

Designing queries

When designing a query there are a number of things you need to think about:

- ☑ What information do you want the query to extract from the database?
- ☑ Which tables will be required in the query?
- ☑ Which fields from those tables will be required?
- ☑ Which (if any) fields will have criteria applied to them to select matching records?
- ☑ Which (if any) fields will be used to sort the matching records?

Queries in the exam

The scenario in the exam will give you details about the information you need to extract from the database. Although you don't need to create query designs, they are a useful way to help you understand how to create the required queries.

An example of query design

In a database of BTEC students there are two related tables, one for students and one for student groups (classes). Imagine you want to design a query that will list all the students in a particular class. A table like this can help you design how the query will work.

Table	Students	Students	Students	Class	Class
Field	ID_Number	First_name	Surname	Class_number	Class_tutor
Criteria				[Enter class number]	
Sort			Ascending		

Wildcards

You can also use **wildcards** in query criteria. For example, to find all the Class tutors whose names begins with 'A', enter 'A*' in the criteria row under the class tutor field.

When using MS Access, putting the criteria in brackets like this will generate a prompt for the user to enter the ID number when the query is run.

Now try this

Design a query for the BTEC students database which will list all the students who have a certain tutor, listed ordered by student ID_number.

Design documentation: test plans

Testing is an important part of the development process as it is essential that you are reasonably sure the database works before people begin to use it.

What do you need to test?

There are a number of things you need to test:

- the validation applied to the database tables (**data testing**)
- the database forms and user interface
- the queries and reports
- that all the required **functionality** works as it should
- that the **usability** and **accessibility** of the user interface is appropriate. For example, is your choice of colours on forms suitable for people with visual impairments?

Create your test plans at the design stage, when you decide what kind of result for each test you are expecting to see when the database is completed.

Data testing

Make sure your test plans include tests of the validation applied to individual fields in a table. For each field, select test data which fits into the following categories:

1 **Normal data** – values which would normally be expected and which should be accepted.

2 **Extreme data** – values at the bounds of what is valid. For example, if a field should only accept values in the range 10 to 20, extreme data would be 9 and 21 (both of which should be rejected), 10 and 20 (both of which should be accepted).

3 **Erroneous data** – data which is completely incorrect such as text entries in numeric fields.

What does a test plan look like?

Create your data test plans in conjunction with your data dictionary.
Here's an example of the data dictionary entry for a field in a Cars table.

Table Name:	Cars
Field name	**Attributes**
No_of_doors	Integer, must be between 2 and 5

Here are the test plan entries for that field:

This column will be completed when the database is actually tested.

Test no.	Table, field	Input data	Expected outcome	Actual outcome
1	Cars, No_of_doors	2	Accepted	
2	Cars, No_of_doors	5	Accepted	
3	Cars, No_of_doors	4	Accepted	
4	Cars, No_of_doors	1	Rejected	
5	Cars, No_of_doors	6	Rejected	
6	Cars, No_of_doors	Two	Rejected	

Tests 4 and 5 also use extreme data – on the borderline of values which should be rejected.

Tests 1 and 2 use extreme data – on the borderline of the acceptable values.

Test 6 uses erroneous data – text values are not allowed in a numeric field.

 Links To revise test plans for other aspects of your database, see page 77.

To revise test plans for other aspects of your database, see page 77.

Now try this

Imagine you have been asked to develop a database with a table of BTEC course units. This has fields for Unit number, Unit name, GLH, Type of assessment, Type of unit. Create a data dictionary and a test plan for this table.

GLH can only be 60, 90 or 120.
Type of assessment is Internal or External.
Type of unit is Mandatory or Optional.

Creating, setting up and maintaining data tables

Once you have completed the design for your database, you can start work on creating the tables.

From data dictionary to table

Your data dictionary is the template for creating the fields in each table. If your data dictionary is correct, creating the tables is easy.

To create a table in MS Access go to the Create menu and choose Table Design.

Remember to set one of the fields as the primary key by clicking the Key icon in the design toolbar.

Remember that fields containing phone numbers should be Text data type, not number, otherwise you won't be able to add a leading zero.

Tutors

Field Name	Data Type
Tutor_ID	AutoNumber
Tutor_Fname	Text
Tutor_Surname	Text
Date_Of_Birth	Date/Time
Phone number	Text

Field Properties

General | Lookup

Field Size	255
Format	
Input Mask	
Caption	
Default Value	
Validation Rule	
Validation Text	
Required	No
Allow Zero Length	Yes
Indexed	No
Unicode Compression	Yes
IME Mode	No Control
IME Sentence Mode	None
Smart Tags	

The AutoNumber data type is useful for a primary key field as Access automatically numbers each record, starting at 1.

Access automatically gives text fields a size of 255 characters. Always change this to a smaller, more appropriate value (and identify this in your data dictionary).

Any field that is a true number must be a numeric data type. This includes fields that you might want to do a calculation with or validate as larger and/or smaller than a certain value.

Field naming

- Be consistent in naming fields. For example, use the same case combinations (for example, upper case for the first character and lower case for the rest).
- It is good practice not to use spaces in your field names. MS Access does allow spaces, but most web-based software does not. Instead, use underscores or capitalisation, e.g. NoOfDoors or No_of_doors.

Maintaining tables

You can always go back and modify the design of a table, but if you have added a lot of data this can cause problems. For example, if you add or modify validation rules Access needs to check that all the existing data on the table meets the new or modified rules. This can take a long time if there are a lot of records in the table. This is one reason why it is important to get the data dictionary correct and follow it when creating your tables.

Now try this

Create a database table for a games database, including fields for Game title, Developer, Release date, Console, Game genre and Price.

Add some data to the table.

Data validation rules: lookup lists

In a field where the valid entries are limited to a few values, the best validation option is a **lookup list**.

Benefits of lookup lists

☑ The user can only choose from a pre-defined list of entries for the fields.

☑ This ensures the entry is valid as no other input to the file is possible.

☑ If you use the Access Form Wizard to create a form based on this table then the Lookup field will automatically be created as a list or combo box.

Using lookup lists with MS Access

 **1** First select the field where you want to use a lookup list, then click the Lookup tab in the Field Properties area.

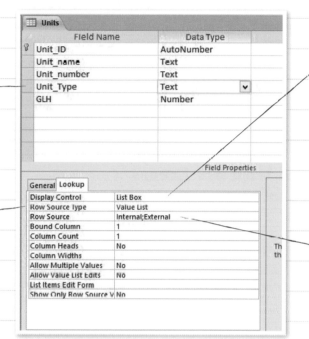

2 You can choose to display the list either in a list box or a combo box. These are quite similar but a combo box has a drop down list, whereas with a list box the list is always visible.

3 A Row Source Type of 'Value List' allows you to type in the values yourself.

4 Enter the values you want the user to select from here, in the 'Row Source' property. Use semicolons to separate the values.

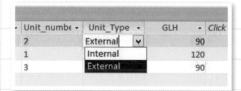

 5 This is how the list box looks in datasheet view.

If you want to pick up the values for the list from another table or query, set the Row Source Type to Table/Query and the Row Source property to the name of the table or query required. The Bound Column property allows you to select the column (field) you want from that table or query.

Now try this

Create a Person table to record people's details (Name, Address, Date of birth, Gender, etc.) and use a lookup list to select the gender (M or F).

If you set up a lookup list in the table design and then create a form based on that table, Access automatically adds a list box to your form.

You can also add list boxes to forms yourself, and use the Lookup wizard to choose if the list values will come from a list you enter or from another table or query.

Data validation rules: comparison and Boolean operators

Where there are more than just a few valid entries for a field, it won't be possible to use a lookup list, but you may be able to use a validation rule.

Validation rules

- Validation rules are very useful where the numeric values entered in a field need to fall within a certain range.

- **Comparison operators** can be used to create rules. These are: > (greater than), < (less than), = (equal to), <= (less than or equal to) and >= (greater than or equal to).

- **Boolean operators** can be used to combine expressions in a validation rule. These are AND and OR.

Other ways to validate input

There are other ways you can validate input.

For example, you can use the Now() function (which represents the current date and time) to ensure a date (such as a birth date) is in the past.

A validation rule of <=Now() will only allow today's date or dates in the past, not future dates.

Default values could be added to cover unknown data, for example an unknown transaction date could have the default value of Now() which would insert the current date.

Using validation rules with MS Access

You can apply a range of types of validation using the Field Properties.

Cars can only have between 2 and 5 doors. You can use a validation rule on this field to ensure that users can only enter values in this range.

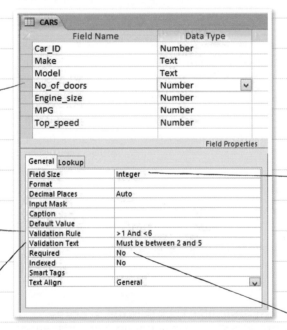

Validation rule: enter the rule here. The 'AND' operator combines the two comparisons together.

Validation text: this is the message that appears if the user enters a value which breaks the rule. It is important that this message is clear, so that the user understands what the problem is.

Data type: setting a data type of integer in the Field Size property ensures that the user cannot enter fractional values such as 4.5

Required: if you set the Required option to yes, this forces the user to make an entry in the field. This can be an important type of validation.

Now try this

Create the table shown in the example above, and add validation rules for Engine_size, MPG and Top_speed.

Very few cars have a top speed of less than 40mph and currently the top speed of the world's fastest road car is 268mph.

Validation rules: input masks

Input masks are useful where a field stores a value which is always the same combination of letters and numbers, or where you want to control the format of the input.

Input masks

Input masks use certain characters and symbols to represent the type of data that can be input.

For example:

0 – the user must enter a digit

9 – the user can optionally enter a digit

L – the user must enter a letter

? – the user can optionally enter a letter

A – the user must enter a letter or digit

> – makes following characters upper case

< – makes following characters lower case

Input mask examples

You can apply an input mask to make sure users enter names (e.g. people's names or place names) properly, for example:

`>L<?????????????`

Using ? allows the user to enter surnames of different lengths. Make sure you include enough question marks to accommodate very long surnames.

It does not matter what case the user types in, the result will automatically have an initial capital followed by all lower case characters.

Characters that you want inserted into the data exactly as they are must be enclosed in double quotes, for example:

`000"-"000`

This requires the user to enter two sets of three digits and automatically places a hyphen (-) between them.

An example of using an input mask for a National Insurance number

Input masks will not let the user type a value that does not match the mask. If they try to nothing happens.

The > symbol makes sure all the letters are upper case.

LL makes the user enter two letters, which are converted to upper case.

Six zeros makes the user enter six numbers.

Field Name	Data Type
Contact_ID	Number
LastName	Text
FirstName	Text
Address	Text
City	Text
NI_number	Text

Field Properties

General | Lookup

Field Size	9
Format	
Input Mask	>LL000000L
Caption	
Default Value	
Validation Rule	...
Validation Text	
Required	No
Allow Zero Length	Yes
Indexed	No
Unicode Compression	Yes
IME Mode	No Control
IME Sentence Mode	None
Smart Tags	

National Insurance (NI) numbers are always in the format of two upper case characters followed by six digits then a final upper case character (e.g. WA749920B).

The final L makes the user complete the NI number with a letter.

Now try this

Imagine you are designing a database table used to record details of different qualifications. You need a field for the qualification number, which is always in the format of three numbers, then a forward slash (/), then four more numbers, then another forward slash, then a final number or upper case letter, e.g. 600/7576/X.

Create an input mask for this field.

Creating relationships

Once you have created the tables in your database, the next step is to create the relationships between the tables.

Creating the relationships between tables

Before creating the relationships, you need to have completed an entity relationship diagram (ERD) and the normalisation process. These will tell you how the tables in the database are related.

- In a one-to-many relationship, to create the link between the tables, take the primary key value from the table on the 'one' side of the relationship and insert it in the corresponding field on the 'many' side as the 'foreign key'.

- If the primary key on the 'one' table uses the AutoNumber data type, the foreign key at the 'many' end of the relationship must have a data type of long integer.

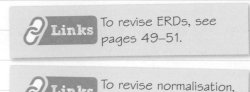 **Links** To revise ERDs, see pages 49–51.

Links To revise normalisation, see pages 55 and 56.

An example of creating relationships

To create relationships in MS Access, click the Relationship icon in the Database Tools menu. Then add the tables you want to create the relationships between. This example shows creating the relationship between the Students and Class tables in a BTEC database.

1 Drag from the primary key field on the 'one' side of the relationship to the foreign key field on the 'many' side. The Edit Relationships box will appear.

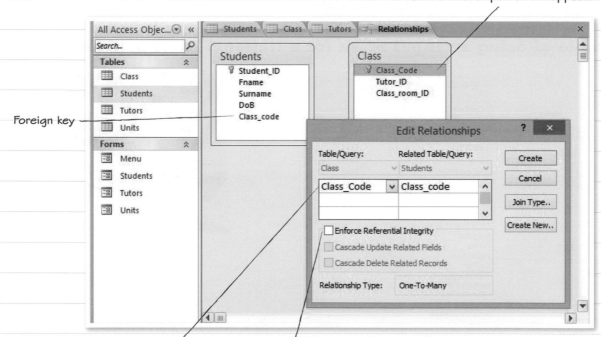

Foreign key

2 The Edit Relationships box should pick up the related fields automatically, but if not choose them here.

3 If you check the 'Enforce Referential Integrity' box, Access won't allow users to create a record on the Student table with a foreign key value that does not exist on the Class table.

Now try this

Create a football database in MS Access with two tables: one for Teams and one for Players, with suitable fields in each table. Make a relationship between the two tables.

Make sure each table contains a primary key field. The Teams table is at the 'one' end, so the primary key on this table will be the foreign key on the Players table at the 'many' end.

Generating output with queries

Queries are powerful tools for extracting data from your database. Users can create their own queries or you can develop queries which run automatically when the user opens a form or report.

Select queries

The Select query is a basic type of query which simply selects the records which match the criteria you define.

How to create a query

To create a query in MS Access, go to the Create menu and click the Query Design icon.
There are five basic steps to running a Select query.

 Add the tables you want to extract the data from.
When using multiple tables in a query the tables need to be related to get meaningful results.

 Select the fields you want displayed in the results.
Drag the fields down from the tables at the top into the query grid at the bottom.

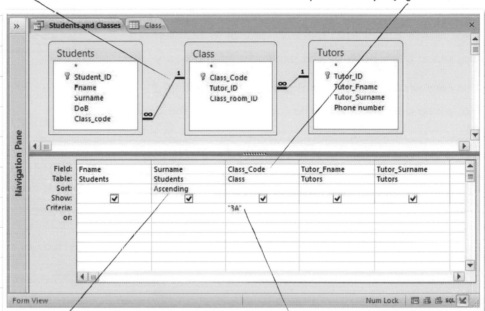

 Select a field to sort the resulting records (optional).
In this query, the results will be sorted in ascending (i.e. alphabetical) order by student surname.

Set the criterion to control the records selected.
Enter the criterion in this row of the query grid. In this example, only those records with 3A in the Class_code field will be selected.

 To run the query, click the Run icon (red exclamation mark) in the toolbar.

Queries using calculated fields

You can add calculated fields in a query. Imagine you have an Orders table with Price and Quantity fields. You could multiply them to get the total cost. In the Field row at the top of the query grid enter **Total: [Price]*[Quantity]** and leave the Table row blank for this field.

You can use the full range of arithmetic operators in your calculated fields: +, −, * and /.

 Now try this

Imagine you want to create a query using the tables in the database shown above. Your query should list all the students with a tutor whose surname is 'Smith', in ascending order of date of birth. What would you enter in the query grid to create this query?

Check your answer by creating the tables and entering a few records in each table. Then create and run your query.

Queries using comparisons and multiple criteria

You can use comparison symbols in queries to find all records with a value greater or smaller than the value you specify for a certain field. You can also combine several criteria to extract exactly the data you want.

Criteria using comparison symbols

The comparison symbols are > (greater than), >= (equal to or greater than), < (less than) and <= (equal to or less than). They can be used with fields that have a numeric data type.

Multiple criteria

In queries with more than one criterion, think about if you want the two (or more) criteria to apply together (AND) or separately (OR). For example, in a car database, do you want the query to return:

1 all cars with 3 doors AND fuel economy of > 50mpg?

In this case, place them both on the same row of the query grid.

2 all the cars which have either 3 doors OR > 50 mpg?

In this case, place one criteria on the 'or:' row below the other one.

Which comparison operator is which?

Here's a helpful way of remembering.

> starts with the greater (larger) end first so it's 'greater than'

< starts with the lesser (smaller) end first, so it's 'less than'.

Examples of queries with multiple criteria

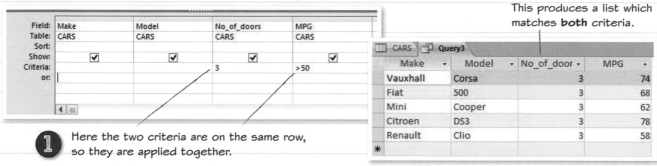

This produces a list which matches **both** criteria.

1 Here the two criteria are on the same row, so they are applied together.

2 Here the two criteria are on different rows, so they are applied separately.

This produces a list that matches **either** criteria, so the list will usually contain more records.

Now try this

Imagine you want to find cars which have an engine size of less than 1600cc and a top speed of over 110mph. Explain how the results would differ if:

(a) you put both these criteria in the Criteria row of the query grid

(b) you put one of the criteria in the Criteria row and one in the 'or': row below this.

Action queries

Action queries make changes to the database rather than just selecting data. In the assessment for this unit you will be provided with sample data. You will need to use action queries to split up the sample data into the different tables of your database, following the design you create.

Using an Action Query in MS Access

The imported sample data will all end up in one table.

🔗 Links To revise how to import data into Microsoft Access, turn to page 82.

1 First create the empty tables that you have specified in your design.

2 Then create a query in design view and add the table with the sample data in it to the query.

3 Now make this table an Append query – go to the Design menu and choose Append.

4 You will be asked which table you want to append (add) the records to. You have to fill up each table one at a time.

This example uses a Games database.

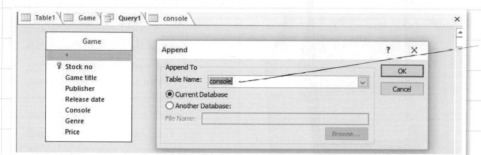

Once you have chosen Append as the type of query, you need to tell it which table you want to add the records to. In this case it is the newly created blank Console table.

5 Now fill in the fields form with the sample data that you want to add to the new table.

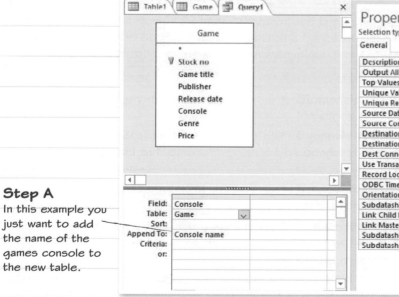

Step A
In this example you just want to add the name of the games console to the new table.

Step B
However, if you append (add) every occurrence of the console name you will get duplicate records. To add only unique records, you need to right click on the query and choose Properties to bring up the Property Sheet for the query. Set Unique Values to Yes.

Step C
When you run this query it will add each unique console name to the new Console table.

6 Run the query by clicking the Run icon in the toolbar.

Now try this

Describe how you can use action queries to split up data into separate tables.

User interface: creating and adjusting forms

You can use forms to create a user interface for your database. Use them to provide menus to allow the user to **navigate** around the system, for data entry and to display the results of queries.

The Form Wizard in MS Access

The easiest way to create forms in MS Access is to use the Form Wizard, which you can access from the Create menu. The wizard will create forms based on either a table or a query.

You can then modify the form created and add more features. For example, you can:

- adjust the layout to better match your designs
- add command buttons – these also run a 'wizard' which allows you to create various **automated functions**, for example to close the form or open another one
- add a **sub-form** (another form within the main form) which displays records from a related table.

Adjusting the layout

You may need to improve the form layout by adjusting field sizes and changing the label text. First open the form in **Design view,** which will display the form in the form editor.

The Controls icon in the toolbar allows you to add a variety of other items to a form. For example, you can add additional text (labels) to help the user understand how to use the form.

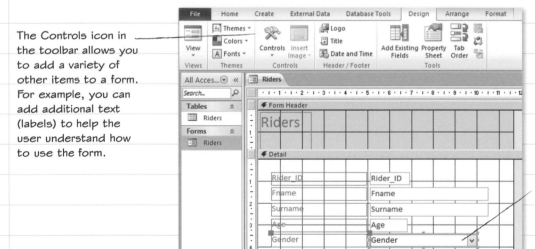

The Form Wizard has created a Gender field that is much larger than it needs to be. Click on it to select it and then use the handles that appear around the edge to change it size.

Creating a data entry form

By default, the Form Wizard creates forms which display all the records in a table. Here's how to create a **data entry form** which is blank when opened, ready to add a new record to the table.

① Create the form with the wizard.

② Then, in design view, click the Property Sheet icon in the toolbar.

③ Select 'Form' in the drop down box at the top of the Property Sheet.

④ Find the Data Entry property underneath and change it to 'Yes'.

Changing form properties

There are many properties of both the whole form and individual fields that you can adjust to change the way the form looks and works.

If you don't want the user to modify the data in a field, you can change the Locked property of the field to Yes and the Enabled property to No so the user can see the data but not change it.

Now try this

Create a data entry form for one of the tables you have already created.

User interface: adding automated features to form

Adding a command button is one way of improving the user interface provided by a form. You can add buttons for the user to perform common tasks such as saving a record or closing the form.

Adding a command button in MS Access

To create a command button on a form:

- open the form in design view
- go to the Design tab of the Form Design Tools menu and click on the Button icon
- then drag a button on the form (this will open the Command Button Wizard).

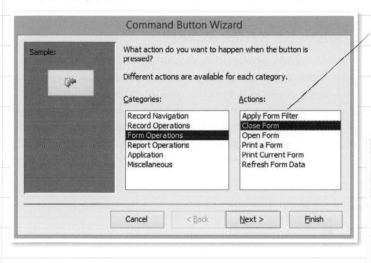

1 In the first step of the Command Button Wizard, select what you want the command button to do.

2 In the second step of the Command Button Wizard, choose the text that appears on the button.

The end result is a form with a button on it which will close the form.

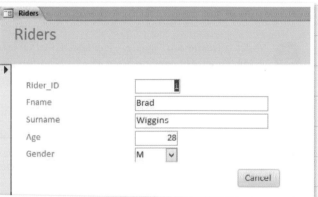

This example shows adding a 'Cancel' command button to close the form.

Add a command button to save a record

You can add a button which saves a record in the same way.

In the first step of the Command Button Wizard, select the Record Operations category and the Save Record action.

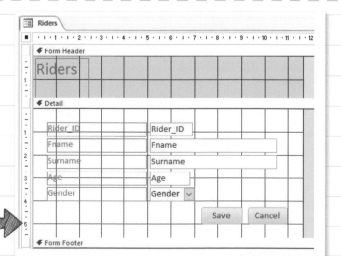

This shows the same form in design view with Save and Cancel buttons added.

Now try this

Create a simple form using the Form Wizard and add Save and Cancel buttons to it.

75

User interface: applying security measures

You need to protect your database using security measures which require users to log on using a password and then give each user access to only those facilities they need to access.

Setting up users and passwords in MS Access

You can create a simple username and password system in Access by following these steps.

1 Create a Users table in the database listing usernames, **passwords** and each user's **access level**, for example like this:

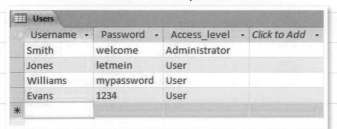

2 Create a form which is not linked to any table with two input text fields for the user to enter their username and password.

Event procedures

An event procedure is a small program that runs when something happens (an event) such as the user clicking a button. You create and edit an event procedure for a button using the property sheet for the button, which you can see when the form is in design view.

3 Add a command button to the form which runs an event procedure that looks up the username and password on the table created in step 1. The form could look something like this:

4 If the username and password combination are not found on the table, the event procedure will need to display a message saying access is denied.

5 If the username and password combination are found, the event procedure will need to display a menu of different options depending on the user's access level.

6 To ensure the login form is shown as soon as the database is opened, create a macro called Autoexec. You must use this name for the macro so that it will open automatically as soon as the database opens. The macro only needs one action, which is to open the login form created in steps 1–3. Here is an example.

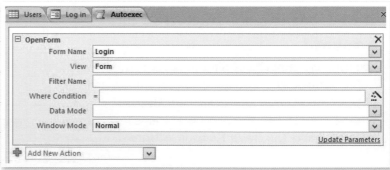

7 Now if you close the database and open it again, the login form will automatically appear and you will need to enter a username and password combination from the users table in order to see the main menu.

Now try this

1 What type of form do you need to create to develop a login system as described on this page?

2 Where are the usernames and passwords stored for the login system?

3 What special name do you have to give a macro to make it run as soon as the database opens?

Testing and refining the database solution

Testing is the essential final step in developing a database. It is important to ensure your database works as it should. Testing links back to the design stage when you should have created a test plan (see page 65).

What do I need to test?

There are a variety of different aspects to your database which you need to test.

1 The data that is input to a table

2 The functionality of forms, queries and reports

Your test plans for these parts of your database need to include tests of all the features and functions of each form, query or report.

3 Referential integrity

If you have used this option in your table relationships (see page 70), test that it works as expected. Make sure you cannot create records at the 'many' end of a relationship that don't have corresponding records at the 'one' end.

4 Security options such as user passwords.

> **Links** To revise data testing, see page 65.

> **Links** To revise security measures, see page 76.

Test documentation checklist

When testing each part of your database you need to complete the test documentation properly.

✓ Use the original test plans and complete the actual **outcomes**.

✓ If the expected and the actual outcomes don't match, record this as an error.

✓ Document what action you took to correct the error.

The development and testing process should be **iterative**. This means that you use the testing outcomes that you record to **improve** and **refine** your database solution in order to ensure an error-free, high-quality product.

Testing a form

Here's an example of a simple data entry form design.

> There is no need to test the validation on the input fields, as this should be done in your data testing of the table, but you should test that the buttons work as expected.

Add a Car

Make	*Make*
Model	*Model*
Doors	*No_of_doors*
Engine Size	*Engine_size*
MPG	*MPG*
Top Speed	*Top_speed*

[Cancel] [Save]

Here are the test plan entries for testing the buttons.

Include a 'Comments and action taken' column so you can explain any tests that need it, and add how you solved errors that you spotted during testing (providing evidence of the iterative process).

Test no.	Table, form	Input data	Expected outcome	Actual outcome	Comments & action taken
1	Cars, Add a car	Click Save button	Record saved, blank form redisplayed		
2	Cars, Add a car	Click Cancel button	Form closed, returned to menu form		

Now try this

1. What are the different aspects of a database that you can test?
2. What test documentation do you need to complete as you do your testing?
3. If you find an error when testing, what should you do?
4. What is the overall purpose of testing?

Evaluating the design process

Evaluating the work you have done is important because it can help you understand how you can improve what you did and the way you did it. This is what learning is all about!

What can I evaluate?

Evaluation involves looking back over your work and asking yourself questions about how well you have fulfilled the requirements of the task. You will need to evaluate the design, development and testing of your database, as well as the final product.

Evaluating the design

You can only evaluate the design after you have developed your database. You can use these questions to help you.

- How well did my design match the final product?
- How useful was my design when developing the product?
- Did I have any problems normalising the data?
- Did I have any problems creating the ERD and data dictionary?
- What was good about my design (its strengths)?
- How could I improve my design to better meet requirements?
- Did my design fully cover the required functionality of the database? Did I miss anything out?

Why do the design first?

Isn't it easier to develop the database first, then do the design?

When creating a simple database it can be tempting to do this. However, this creates two problems:

- It is hard to evaluate the design if it has been created after the database is developed.
- You need to develop design skills which can be applied to more complex situations and this will only happen if you practise and get in the habit of creating the design first.

Tips for your evaluation

Writing an evaluation can be hard, so here are a couple of tips:

Keep a design and development diary

Taking notes while you design and create a database will help you a lot when you come to do the evaluation. Note down things you found hard and problems you came across. Without notes it can be hard to remember the earlier stages of the design and development.

Make sure you cover the following points

When evaluating each aspect of your work you need to do three things:

- Explain the good points.
- Explain the bad points.
- Draw a reasoned conclusion.

 Links To revise evaluating the development and testing process, see page 79.

Now try this

Write up these diary notes as the first part of an evaluation.

 Turn the notes into the 'story' of what you did and reflect on how well the process went and how you could have done it better.

Diary notes – design stage

Mon: Highlighted the repeating groups in the raw data. Attempted the normalisation process but got confused at the 3rd normal form stage.

Tue: Read the database scenario again and drafted the ERD. Went through the normalisation process again and compared it with my draft ERD – think it's correct now.

Wed   Drew final version of ERD and started work on the data dictionary.

Evaluating the development and testing process

Software development is not easy and it is likely that you will come across a number of issues as you develop databases. Here are some questions to ask to help you decide what to include in your evaluation of the development and testing phases of your database task.

Evaluating the development process

- **How did the development go?** Think about the problems you came across and what you found difficult.

  For example, did you have any problems getting the queries or forms to work as required?

- **How well does the final product meet the users' needs?** As a learner your 'users' will mostly be imaginary but you should still think about whether your database would meet all the users' needs.

  For example, what features and options would be very useful to a real user that you didn't have time to add?

- **What do others think of my database?** It's difficult to be critical of things you created so getting other people's feedback can be enlightening. You can't do this in the exam, so use your practice activities to gain an idea of the sort of things users might like or dislike about your databases.

The iterative process

Software development is usually an **iterative process**. This means you develop something, try it out, find some issues, do further development to resolve the issues, then try it out again.

You use this kind of iterative process to refine and improve software in stages.

In your evaluation consider how effective the iteration process has been. Is your database fully refined or would further iterations refine it further?

Evaluating the testing

- Did I fully complete the **testing records**?
- Did I include **screen shots** and comment on the results?
- Which tests were met successfully?
- Which failed tests were not resolved?
- Where the actual result did not match the expected result, did I fully investigate and comment on the reasons for this?
- Did I use the **testing outcomes** to improve my database?

Make sure when writing an evaluation that any points you make are supported by evidence from the actual database/scenario.

Evaluating the final product

- What are the **strengths** and **weaknesses** of the final product?
- Is it **fit for** its intended **purpose**?
- Is it complete and fully functional?
- To what extent does it meet the **functionality requirements**?
- Is the user interface **intuitive** and **easy to use**?
- Is the database easy for others to **maintain**?
- Are there any **constraints** (restrictions) on how the database can be used?
- What will I do differently next time?

Checklist for your evaluation

 1 How well did my design match the final product?

 2 What went well during development and what problems did I have?

3 How did I overcome the problems?

 **Evaluation**

 7 If I developed the database again, what would I do differently?

4 How clear and easy to use is the user interface?

 6 If I had more time, how could I improve the database?

 5 How effective was the testing at uncovering issues? Have I tested my database enough?

Now try this

Write a list of headings you can use to help you structure an evaluation of your database.

About your set task

The Unit 2 assessment is based on the completion of a set task. This means that you will sit at a computer to complete a series of activities which make up the set task. These activities involve designing, developing, testing and evaluating a database solution for a given scenario.

How long have I got?

- In total you have **10 hours**.
- The 10 hours are split up into a number of sessions, which will be decided by your teacher.
- The sessions must be completed in 1 week.
- For example, your sessions might be split up like this:
  - Monday – 2 hours morning
  - Tuesday – 2 hours morning, 2 hours afternoon
  - Wednesday – 2 hours morning
  - Thursday – 2 hours morning.

When will I take the assessment?

- The date of the assessment is set by Pearson. There is one assessment in December/January and another in May/June.
- You can only retake the assessment once.

The activities and suggested time allocations

The activities are **always the same**. You will always be asked to complete the six activities shown in the table.

The table also lists the time allocations suggested for each activity.

Set task activities	No. of marks	Suggested time allocations
Processing the scenario	N/A	5 minutes
Activity 1: Entity relationship diagram	8 marks	1 hour
Activity 2: Data dictionary	8 marks	1 hour
Activity 3: Design specification	6 marks	1 hour 45 minutes
Activity 4: Testing plan	6 marks	1 hour
Activity 5: Database development	26 marks	4 hours
Activity 6: Evaluation of your database solution	12 marks	1 hour
Proofread	N/A	10 minutes
Totals	**66 marks**	**10 hours**

You get nearly one-third of the total marks for Activity 5 (Database development and testing). You must plan your time carefully so you do not spend too much time on Activities 1–4.

The suggested timings allow about 5 hours for the design (Activities 1–4). Depending on your database software skills, you might need more time for Activity 5. If so, consider limiting the time you spend on the design to around 4 hours.

Practising the activities is the best way to find out how much time you need to allow for each one!

The set task brief

While the activities are always the same, the scenario in the set task brief is different for each assessment. You won't know which scenario you will receive when you take your assessment, so make sure you practise your skills by completing the six tasks for a number of different scenarios.

Now try this

Look at the table of activities. Rank each activity from 1 to 6 based on how confident you are with that activity.

Activity 1 ☐   Activity 2 ☐   Activity 3 ☐

Activity 4 ☐   Activity 5 ☐   Activity 6 ☐

You can use this list to help you prioritise your revision.

The set task brief

Your set task brief will provide a scenario that you will need to consider carefully when completing the six activities.

The set task brief consists of:

- a scenario which describes the database application
- a list of the features and database outputs which are required
- some sample data, which is provided in an electronic file.

Reading the brief

Always read the brief carefully and make notes on the clues it contains about the structure of the database.

Task scenario

Here is an exemplar task scenario to help you understand the things you need to think about when reading your brief.

DO NOT WRITE IN THIS AREA

You have been asked to create a database for a slimming club. People who join the club are allocated a mentor who meets them weekly, discusses their diet and exercise regime and weighs them. The mentors who work with the club members are:

- Jenny Smith (female)
- Simon Jones (male)
- Sally Carr (female)
- Anita Patel (female).

Members are always allocated a mentor who is the same gender as they are.

When the results of the weekly weigh-in are entered for a member the total weight they have lost is updated. All weights are recorded in kilograms (kg).

You need to:
- design a database structure that:
  - includes member, mentor and weekly weigh-in data
  - avoids unnecessary duplication
  - validates data input to ensure integrity.
- create a robust database with a suitable user interface which will allow users to:
  - input new members and allocate them to a mentor
  - input the results of weekly weigh-ins
  - input new mentors.
- provide database outputs which show:
  - all the members allocated to a specified mentor
  - all the weekly weigh-in results for a specified member
  - a report listing all the weigh-ins for a specified week, ranked by weight lost (compared to starting weight)
  - a report listing a specified member's weigh-ins, with the difference between each week's weight and their target weight shown.

This data will be repeated in the sample data file. BUT make a note that it looks as if it belongs in a separate table.

Make a note that this will require some input validation.

Make a note that this will require a calculation to be done when the data is input.

This is an important clue to the tables required: **Members**, **Mentors** and **Weigh-in**.

You will need to create forms for these inputs.

These database outputs will be created using queries, so make a note that this is the list of queries required.

Now try this

Complete this list of all the things you need to do to carry out the tasks listed in the example task scenario. Write your list in the order you need to carry out the tasks. For example:

1 Design the database structure, including normalising the data and drawing an ERD.
2 Create a data dictionary for the tables defined in the ERD, including any validation.
3 …

The data

In the assessment, after the set task brief, there will be a table showing some sample raw data for the database you will be creating. You will also be provided with the sample data in electronic format.

The sample data

- The data you are provided with for the assessment is raw data – it won't have been normalised or split into separate tables.
- You need to import the data into your database software.
- DO NOT type the data in. This would waste far too much time.
- Once you have completed your database design, you can divide up the data into the correct tables.

Importing the data

The sample data file will be provided as a 'CSV' file, which is a type of text file. To import the data into Microsoft Access:

1 Open or create a database.

2 From the External Data menu, choose Text file.

3 Find the file you need to import and choose to import it into a new table.

4 Follow the steps in the Text Import Wizard. Remember to check if the first row of the data contains field names.

Practise this process until you are confident you can do it quickly and correctly as importing the data is crucial to being able to complete the assessment.

Sample data

This is sample data relating to the exemplar task scenario given on page 80.

> This sample data shows three slimming club members with three weekly weigh-ins each. You will get more data than this in the assessment – probably about 30 records.

> Use highlighter pens to identify the repeating data.

Member name	Member Age	Member gender	Target weight (kg)	Starting_ weight (kg)	Mentor name	Mentor gender	Week	Weight (kg)
Hazel Williams	42	F	75	95	Jenny Smith	F	1	95
Hazel Williams	42	F	75	95	Jenny Smith	F	2	90
Hazel Williams	42	F	75	95	Jenny Smith	F	3	90
Smita Shah	36	F	80	105	Jenny Smith	F	1	105
Smita Shah	36	F	80	105	Jenny Smith	F	2	100
Smita Shah	36	F	80	105	Jenny Smith	F	3	98
Clive Hanson	47	M	70	88	Simon Jones	M	1	88
Clive Hanson	47	M	70	88	Simon Jones	M	2	85
Clive Hanson	47	M	70	88	Simon Jones	M	3	83

> The member's name and details repeat in each or their records.

> The mentor's name and details also repeat.

Now try this

Copy this data into an Excel spreadsheet (or make up your own) and then save it as a CSV file. Practise importing the CSV file into an Access database using the Text Import Wizard.

Activity 1: entity relationship diagram (normalisation)

For Activity 1 you need to create an entity relationship diagram (ERD) for the data provided. The ERD is created in conjunction with normalising the data, and splitting it into separate tables.

The normalisation process

1 The first stage is to examine the raw data and identify repeating data.

2 Then remove repeating data to another table.

3 Split any fields which are not 'atomic'. (Remember that atomic means cannot be split up.)

4 Add a primary key field to each table, as the original data did not have one.

 Links Refresh your memory of normalisation by turning to pages 55 and 56.

Why is normalisation important?

- If you read the task brief carefully and inspect the sample data as explained on page 82, you should have a pretty good idea of the different tables required.
- BUT make sure you provide a proper explanation of the normalisation process to show that you understand how to do it.
- Normalising the raw data is part of the assessment requirements and is a useful way of checking your tables and making sure your database is as efficient as possible.

Sample response extract

In the raw data for the slimming club database, the details of each member repeat.

You therefore need to move them to a separate Member table.

Member table

Member_ID	First_name	Surname	Age	Gender	Target_weight_kg	Starting_weight_kg	Mentor_ID
1	Hazel	Williams	42	F	75	95	1
2	Smita	Shah	36	F	80	105	1
3	Clive	Hanson	47	M	70	00	2

Add a primary key field.

Split the member name field into First_name and Surname to ensure the data is 'atomic'.

Identify each member's mentor by including the Mentor_ID (the foreign key) in the Member table.

Sample response extract

Mentor table

Mentor_ID	Mentor_first_name	Menor_surname	Mentor_gender
1	Jenny	Smith	F
2	Simon	Jones	M

The names and genders of the mentors also repeat in the raw data.

So you need to move them to a separate Mentor table.

Add a primary key for the Mentor table and split the mentor name field.

Now try this

The remaining, non-repeating data is the data about the weigh-ins that each slimming club member has every week.

1 Draw a separate Weigh-in table for the slimming club database.

2 Explain how each weigh-in will link to the member who is weighed.

Use the remaining fields from page 82 and add any other necessary fields (primary key and foreign key).

Activity 1: entity relationship diagram (drawing the ERD)

Once you have normalised the data you can draw the ERD.

Steps of drawing an ERD

1 First draw the entities and the relationships between them.

2 Then decide what kind of relationship exists between the entities and add that to your diagram.

Most relationships are of the one-to-many type. But make sure you identify which is the 'one' end and which is the 'many' end.

> **⊘ Links** To revise entity relationship diagrams and types of relationship, see pages 50 and 51.

Sample response extract

> In the slimming club database there are three entities.

> You know from the normalisation process that the Member table is linked to both the Mentor table and the Weigh-in table.

Sample response extract

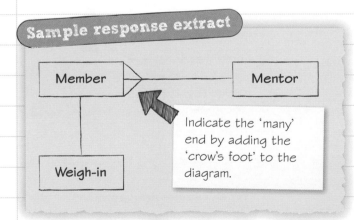

> Indicate the 'many' end by adding the 'crow's foot' to the diagram.

Questions to help you decide on the type of relationship

- For the relationship between the Member and Mentor tables, ask: 'How many mentors does each member have?'

Answer: each member only has one mentor.

- To check this, ask: 'How many Members does each Mentor look after?'

Answer: each mentor could look after many members.

This shows that the Member table is the 'many' end and the Mentor table is the 'one' end.

Now try this

The ERD in Step 2 above is incomplete.

1 What is the type of relationship between the Member table and the Weigh-in table?

2 Complete the ERD by adding the crow's foot at the 'many' end.

> Another way to check which end is which is to see which table has the foreign key inserted in it. This will be the 'many' end of the relationship.

Activity 2: data dictionary

The second activity is to create a data dictionary for the database you are designing. It will need to provide details of all the tables that your entity relationship diagram, created for activity 1, has defined. You will be provided with a template to create the data dictionary.

Data dictionary checklist

☑ You must make a copy of the data dictionary table, one for each table you identified in your ERD.

☑ Make sure you use the same table names as in your ERD.

☑ Remember to include all the fields for each table that your normalisation process identified.

☑ In the Attributes column you need to include information about each field, including:

- if the field is a primary or foreign key
- the data type of the field, for example numeric (integer, decimal, etc.), text, date, currency
- any validation rules that should be applied to the field.

Getting it right!

Before you start work on your data dictionary, make sure that your ERD and normalisation are correct.

Creating the data dictionary follows on directly from these design items so, if they are correct, producing the data dictionary is relatively straightforward.

The assessment information advises spending an hour on the data dictionary, which should be more than enough, so spend extra time on the normalisation and ERD if needed.

 Links To revise creating a data dictionary, see page 57.

To revise creating a data dictionary, see page 57.

Sample response extract

Data dictionary for the Member table

Table Name:	Members
Field name	Attributes
Member_ID	Primary key, 'autonumber' field generated by the software
F_name	Text data type, 25 characters, no validation
Surname	Text data type, 25 characters, no validation
Age	Integer data type, must be between 18 and 99
Gender	Text data type, 1 character, must be M or F
Target_weight_kg	Integer data type, must be between 50 and 120
Starting_weight_kg	Integer data type, must be between 75 and 200
Mentor_ID	Foreign key, numeric data type (integer), must exist on the Mentor table.

 Use a consistent naming convention when naming tables and fields, for example initial capitals with an underscore replacing spaces.

 Make sure your data types are correct. For example, remember that a phone number should use a text rather than numeric data type.

Now try this

Create data dictionaries for the Mentor and Weigh-in tables for the slimming club database.

Activity 3: design specification – the user interface (forms)

The user interface will consist of forms you create to allow users to carry out required functions.

What do I need to design?

- The assessment task does not state exactly what forms the user interface will need, so you need to use a little imagination.
- You need to create:
  - a menu form to allow users to access the input forms and queries
  - input forms.

Don't be tempted to spend too much time on this activity. The recommended time is 1hr 45mins.

Use the 'specification document' template that is provided and create simple but clear outline designs for each form.

The task brief for the slimming club database (see page 81) asked for:
- two input forms: to input new users and allocate them to a mentor; to input weekly weigh-in results
- four 'database outputs' – you will need to use queries to create these.

This student's answer shows a menu form and a new member input form for the slimming club.

Sample response extract

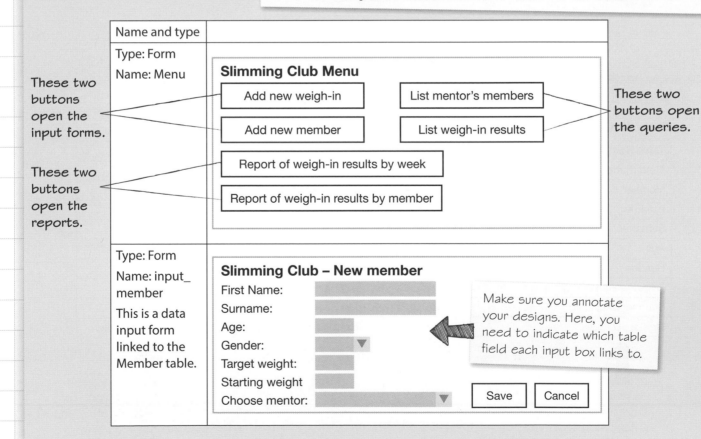

These two buttons open the input forms.

These two buttons open the reports.

These two buttons open the queries.

Name and type	
Type: Form Name: Menu	**Slimming Club Menu** Add new weigh-in List mentor's members Add new member List weigh-in results Report of weigh-in results by week Report of weigh-in results by member
Type: Form Name: input_member This is a data input form linked to the Member table.	**Slimming Club – New member** First Name: Surname: Age: Gender: Target weight: Starting weight Choose mentor: Save Cancel

Make sure you annotate your designs. Here, you need to indicate which table field each input box links to.

Now try this

Create designs for forms for the slimming club database:
(a) to allow users to add new weigh-ins
(b) to allow users to add new mentors.

 Links To revise user interface design, see page 62.

Activity 3: design specification – the user interface (queries)

As well as the forms, you also need to provide designs for the queries.

How to design a query

One of the 'database outputs' the slimming club brief (see page 81) asks for is:

• **all the weekly weigh-in results for a specified member**.

The brief mentions the weigh-in and the member so you will need fields from both the Weigh-in and Member tables. This output requires the results for a specified member, so use the Member_ID as a criterion so the query only returns results for the member selected. Using MemberID ensures the correct member is returned by the query. An alternative design could search by F_name and Surname.

Sample response extract

Query design

Name and type						
Type: Query Name: List_weights						
	Table	Member	Member	Member	Weigh-in	Weigh-in	Weigh-in
	Field	Member_ID	F_name	Surname	Member_ID	Week_no	Weight_kg
	Criteria	[Enter member ID]					
	Sort					Ascending	

Using square brackets will create a prompt, using the message within the brackets.

Using this foreign key from the Weigh-in table will link to the Member table.

This will ensure the data is displayed sorted by week number.

Now try this

The slimming club task brief (see page 81) asks for another output which shows:

• **all the members allocated to a specified mentor**.

Create a query design for this output.

Read the brief carefully. The wording here gives you a strong clue about which tables you need to include in your query.

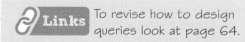
To revise how to design queries look at page 64.

Activity 3: design specification – the user interface (reports)

Some of the outputs required for your assessment will be in the form of reports. Reports can sometimes use data directly from a table, but more often they are based on a query that brings together data from several tables.

How to design a report

The first part of designing a report is often to design the query. In MS Access, you will usually create your reports using the Report Wizard which does a lot of the hard work for you. The main things you need to decide when using the wizard are:

- which table or query will supply the data for the report
- how you want data grouped within the report
- how you want the data sorted in the report
- what layout you want for the report.

The first report the slimming club brief (see page 81) asks for is:

- **a report listing all the weigh-ins for a specified week, ranked by weight lost (compared to starting weight).**

The query that provides the data for this report will use the Member and Weigh-in tables. The criterion will be the week number, which the user will enter.

The weight lost needs to be calculated by subtracting the current weight from the starting weight.

Sample response extract

Query design

Name and type								
Type: Query Name: Weight_ lost	**Table**	Member	Member	Member	Member	Weigh-in	Weigh-in	Weigh-in	
	Field	Member_ ID	F_name	Surname	Starting_ weight_ kg	Member_ ID	Weight_ kg	Week	Loss:[Starting_ weight_kg]– [Weight_kg]
	Criteria							[Enter week]	
	Sort								Ascending

Report design

Weekly Weight Loss Report   The report is grouped by week number.   The report is sorted by weight lost.

Week number: N

Member name		Starting weight	Current weight	Weight lost
Xxxxxx	xxxxxxx	nnnn kg	nnnn kg	nnnn kg
Xxxxxx	xxxxxxx	nnnn kg	nnnn kg	nnnn kg

Now try this

The second report the slimming club task brief (see page 81) asks for:

- **a report listing a specified member's weigh-ins, with the difference between each week's weight and their target weight shown.**

Create a query design and a report design for this output.

The query should prompt the user to enter the member ID or name and it will need to calculate the difference between the member's current weight and their target weight. The report should group the data by the member.

 Links To revise designing reports, see page 63.

 Links To revise how to include calculations in your queries, look at page 71.

Activity 4: testing plan

Your test plan should list all the tests you will carry out for all the tables, queries and forms.

Test plans checklist

✓ Create your test plans at the design stage, although you won't do the actual testing until you have developed the database.

✓ List the tests using the template provided in the 'Test log and evaluation document'.

✓ Include tests for the validation you have added to the fields in each table.

✓ Also include tests to check that the forms and queries work as they should.

Test data checklist

✓ In your test data for numeric fields, include normal, extreme (testing the limits of allowed values) and erroneous (totally wrong) data.

✓ In your test plans for forms, include tests for any buttons you have added.

✓ In your test plans for queries, include tests for different criteria values.

 Links To revise test plans and data testing, see page 65.

Sample response extract

Test plan for the Member table

Use the 'Test log and evaluation document' provided to create your test plan, adding rows as necessary.

This sample answer shows part of a learner's test plan for the Member table. It is based on the data dictionary on page 82.

Test No.	Purpose of test	Test data	Expected result	Actual result	Comment/actions
	Tests for the Member table, Age field				
1	Normal data	28	Accepted		
2	Extreme data	18	Accepted		
3	Extreme data	17	Rejected		
4	Extreme data	99	Accepted		
5	Extreme data	100	Rejected		
6	Erroneous data	Twenty	Rejected		
	Tests for the Member table, Gender field				Implemented using a lookup table
1	Normal data	M	Accepted		
2	Normal data	F	Accepted		

The extreme values test the boundaries of what is accepted and rejected.

 Because this field is implemented using a lookup table, only the values M and F can be selected.

 Remember to leave the 'Actual result' column blank at design stage. When completing the assessment, have a version of your test plan in the design section with no actual results. Then when you have developed the database, make a copy of the table and fill in the actual results.

Now try this

Create test plans for the Mentor and Weigh-in tables.

Activity 5: database development

Once you have completed the design, it is time to create the database.

The steps in developing the database

1 Create the tables.

2 Import the data file provided.

3 Split the data file up into the different tables.

4 Create the relationships between the tables.

5 Create the queries.

6 Create the forms.

What evidence do I need to provide?

The evidence for this activity is a series of screenshots. Make sure your screenshots provide a clear 'story' of your development process, and annotate them to explain what they show.

You do not need to have a screenshot for every single step in developing each item. Just show the design view and the completed item for each table, form, query etc.

Sample response extract

The Member table

This is the Member table in datasheet view. You can see I have used a lookup table for the Gender field.

Member_ID ▾	F_name ▾	Surname ▾	Age ▾	Gender ▾	Target_weig ▾	Starting_we ▾	Men
1	Hazel	Williams	52	F	75	97	
2	Smita	Shah	36	F	80	108	
3	Clive	Hanson	47	M	70	90	
*	(New)						

This is the table in design view.

Field Name	Data Type
Member_ID	AutoNumber
F_name	Short Text
Surname	Short Text
Age	Number
Gender	Short Text
Target_weight_kg	Number
Starting_weight_kg	Number
Mentor_ID	Number
Date of birth	Date/Time

Field Properties

General | Lookup

Display Control	List Box
Row Source Type	Value List
Row Source	M;F
Bound Column	1
Column Count	1
Column Heads	No
Column Widths	
Allow Multiple Values	No
Allow Value List Edits	Yes
List Items Edit Form	
Show Only Row Source V	No

For the Member table, you would also include screenshots showing the validation added to the Age and Target_weight_kg fields.

The Member_ID field is the Primary key, it has AutoNumber data type so each record gets a unique key.

Mentor_ID is the foreign key which links to the Mentor table.

You can see here how I have set up the list box for the Gender field, with only the values M and F in it.

Now try this

Develop some of the forms, queries and/or reports you designed in the 'Now try this' tasks on pages 86–88. Create annotated screenshots showing what you have done.

Activity 6: evaluation of your database solution

The final step in the assessment is to write an evaluation of the process of designing, developing and testing the database.

What should the evaluation include?

- Include both the good and bad points of the design, development and testing process.
- Don't be afraid to say what went wrong and what might be the flaws in your database.

 To revise the evaluation process turn to pages 78 and 79.

Some questions to address in your evaluation

- Did your final product match the design?
- Did you discover flaws in your design during implementation?
- Were there any aspects of the design, development or testing you had problems with?
- What further work would the database need before it could be used for real?

Preparing for the evaluation

By the time you get to this last activity you could well be running short of time. Also, it may be difficult to remember some of the issues you had in the earlier activities (which you may have done several days previously).

To make sure you cover everything, keep the document you will use for your evaluation open throughout the assessment and, when you think of things you should put in the evaluation, make a note of them in the document.

Point, Evidence, Explain

You can use the P.E.E. technique to structure what you write in your evaluation.

 1 Make a **Point**.   **2** Provide **Evidence**.   **3** **Explain** why this is important.

You might find it helpful to use a table to remind you how you use this technique.

Point	Evidence	Explain
My user interface is easy to use.	The layout is consistent, all the fields are clearly labelled and Save and Cancel buttons are provided.	Consistent and clear labelling helps the user know how to use the form. The Cancel button is important so that the users can back out of the update if needed.
My database needs further work to make it really useful.	There is no facility to draw graphs from the data on weigh-ins.	Members are likely to want a graph of their weight loss over time.

Sample response extract

I did all the tests and found no errors.

This is just a simple point. It does not provide any evidence or explanation.

This makes the point, provides evidence (says what the learner did and did not test) and explains the issues that the lack of testing can cause.

Improved response extract

I did all the tests in my test plan and I found no errors. Due to time limitations, I did not test the queries, forms and reports. I only tested the input validation on the tables. This means that I have not tested the database thoroughly enough and I should have created more test data to cover these aspects of the database, where errors may well exist.

Now try this

Choose one section (design, development or testing) of your work and write an evaluation of it.

Answers

Unit 1: Information Technology Systems

Please note: these are example correct answers. Other correct answers are possible.

1. Digital devices 1

(a) Mobile device such as a tablet.

(b) It has a built-in battery and is designed to run off the battery for long periods of time without charging. Tablets are also often built in with a mobile broadband connection to allow internet access on the go.

2. Digital devices 2

Barcode scanner and magnetic stripe reader.

3. Uses of digital devices

A barcode scanner can be used to identify products. The scanner will read the barcodes on the products and look up the products' information, such as the price.

A magnetic stripe reader can be used for payment. The reader can read the magstripe found on the back of credit and debit cards so that this payment method can be used.

4. Input and output devices

A graphics tablet would be useful to Marit as it allows her to produce a drawing in a similar way to using a pen and paper. She uses a stylus on a tablet in order to produce illustrations with greater accuracy than with a mouse. A scanner is also a useful input device for Marit as she can scan photos or illustrations into her computer so she can then edit them.

A monitor is important for Marit as without it she wouldn't be able to see what she is doing on the computer, such as the illustrations she is working on. A printer would also be helpful so she can produce hard copy prints of the work she has created, allowing her to provide clients with proofs before going to print.

5. Devices for accessibility and data processing

A Braille embosser will allow Marcus to print out his work in Braille so he will be able to read it as a hard copy.

Speakers are another peripheral device that will help Marcus use his IT system. Used along with screen-reading software, it will allow him to know what is on screen even without being able to see it.

6. Storage devices

USB sticks have a relatively low storage capacity when compared to external SSDs and HDDs. This would be a problem for transferring videos and graphics, as these types of file require a very large storage capacity. USB sticks can also be somewhat easy to break – for example they have a finite number of writes. This would be a problem if the user is constantly removing and adding new files, although SSDs also have this problem.

7. Types of operating system

Modern operating systems often require computers with powerful hardware capabilities. If your computer has limited CPU speed, RAM capacity and HDD read/write speed then you will find the entire system may run very slowly, which reduces productivity. Operating system performance can also be negatively impacted by malware such as viruses and worms. The malicious software programs can slow down performance or even damage files and stop the operating system from working at all. Malicious software may also result in a user's data being inaccessible, or their identity being compromised. A final factor that can affect performance of the operating system is virtual memory. This is memory that is in main storage rather than RAM. A PC uses RAM to store data that is currently being worked on, so if a PC runs out of RAM it uses virtual memory – but this can be slow as it might be constantly moving data between main memory and storage (known as thrashing). Improving the hardware, such as by adding more RAM and/or a storage device with faster access times, reduces response times and reduces the need to use virtual memory.

8. The role of the operating system

One way in which an operating system manages memory is by allocating memory to processes. Each process that must be completed requires memory to be assigned to it and the operating system ensures that this happens. The operating system will also un-allocate memory. This means that when a process is no longer running the OS will free up that memory so it can be used by other processes.

9. User interfaces

Completing tasks using a command line interface can be much quicker for knowledgeable and experienced users who know the commands, like Rahul. If Rahul is using an older computer the command line interface would also be useful as this type of user interface uses much fewer resources, like memory and processor power, than other interfaces, like a GUI.

10. Utility software

A disk defragmenter is a utility tool that reorganises data on a hard disk so that files are no longer fragmented across the disk. This will improve disk access time and so improve the time it takes to read and write to the hard disk. As a result Jessica would notice less time spent waiting for disk activity. Anti-virus software is a utility tool that identifies malware on a system and removes them. This could improve the performance of Jessica's computer system, as many malware programs are designed to damage a computer and reduce its performance. Malware could use the computer's processing power and internet connection as part of a BotNet, or steal Jessica's data.

11. File types

JPG files would be beneficial to Kasim as they use compression to reduce the size of files so that they can be easily shared over the internet. BMP files would be an alternative as this is an uncompressed file format so Kasim's photography images would retain a very high quality.

12. Application software

One of the benefits of open source software is that it is free to use. Proprietary software is often expensive so the saving Seth makes may be quite significant. Additionally, open source software allows users to read and modify the source code for the program. This means that if the program is missing a feature that Seth requires, he could hire a developer to make modifications to add this extra functionality. This will ensure that the software will do exactly what he needs it to. Although the open source software will be free to use, Seth needs to consider the potential costs involved in adapting the software to his needs and in obtaining support should it be needed.

13. Emerging technologies

Liam needs to consider how much data his new loyalty card scheme is going to generate. If he is tracking the buying habits of every customer at every petrol station then that data soon begins to mount up.

In order to work out how to steer his business, Liam needs to be able to analyse the data and match it up with the customers' demographics (i.e. the statistical data of his customers, including information such as average age, income, education, etc.). Without any form of loyalty scheme, there is little demand from Liam in terms of data storage and very little information needs sharing between sites. With the introduction of his loyalty card scheme Liam will have to consider how his current data storage is going to cope and how he is going to effectively analyse this data. Also his network infrastructure must be able to cope with the needs of this data-rich system.

14. Choosing an IT system

One consideration is cost. Personal computers have a wide range in costs, with high-end gaming PCs potentially costing thousands of pounds. Benjamin must make sure he knows his friend's budget before he makes a recommendation. Specification is another consideration. Video games often have minimum and recommended specification requirements for the system used to play them. He must know the requirements for the games his friend wants to play and make sure the PC meets at least the minimum requirements.

15. Wired connection methods

As Meera is developing new products, attention to detail is going to be key. To get the best possible quality out of the system, Meera needs to ensure the connection is capable of supporting the 4k resolution. HDMI is a very common digital technology used to interconnect display equipment, and it supports 4k resolutions – it also has the added bonus of carrying sound if needed. Additionally, the screen is a touch screen, which is an input device. USB would be a good choice here and it is likely that the screen uses USB to connect the touch-screen element of the display as this allows data to flow in both directions and is commonly used for things like input devices.

16. Wireless connection methods

WiFi will allow Shaheera to set up a home network without having to have cables across her house which could cause a tripping hazard. It also has good data transfer speeds (compared to other wireless networking options) and so she can still make full use of her home broadband connection.

17. Features of different networks

A personal area network is a network between devices within a very short range, whereas a local area network can be spread over a whole site. Because James is trying to connect his devices in a very small range for simple sharing, and the devices stated are likely to be carried by James, a PAN is more appropriate.

18. Network choice and performance

Jane should be looking for components that are going to provide her with the ability to move files between devices quickly. It is likely her needs include larger files, and she may continue to expand into video in the future. She should consider a combination of 802.11ac wireless which allows the flexibility to move around and benefit from high speeds combined with a gigabit over copper network which gives rapid desktop-based speeds at a reasonable cost overall.

19. Protocols

POP3 is a protocol for receiving emails where the messages are downloaded to a personal computer. This means they will only be accessible on the device they were downloaded to but are available offline. IMAP is a protocol where emails are synced with the mail server so that Alex can access her emails on multiple devices as long as she has an active internet connection, so this protocol would be more beneficial for Alex.

20. Data transmission issues

Bandwidth is the rate at which data can be transferred over a network, whereas latency is the time it takes for the data to reach its destination. So if you are playing a game which will need to send a lot of data, a high bandwidth is needed, but if you need a fast response to show updates from other players then low latency is required.

21. Features of online systems

Using cloud storage means that Kyle's files will be uploaded to the cloud when saved and downloaded when needed. This can make heavy use of his bandwidth, which is usually limited on mobile broadband connections, so Kyle would have to consider whether he has sufficient bandwidth allowances. Kyle's files that are stored on the cloud are also potentially less secure, as a hacker could gain access to his files and misuse them for purposes such as identity fraud. This could be done more easily as his files are stored on public servers. Although security is likely to be strong, it is never perfect.

22. Using online systems

One of the factors Kasia must consider is cost. Cloud services are often free, although subscription based products are available, often with enhanced feature sets and support packages. Those that aren't are usually paid for by subscription. This reduces the initial payment but Kasia must ensure she can afford the ongoing payments and ensure the product continues to add value to her business. In the long term it may result in costing more than the upfront costs of non-cloud based systems. Another factor is the features available. Cloud-based services may not have exactly the same features as the standalone software applications she is used to and therefore they may not meet her needs.

23. Online communities: methods of communicating

Social media is a good way for Amit to get involved with an online community. He could join a group dedicated to football or his favourite team to take part in discussions with others. Another method would be a blog. He could read articles written in the blog and comment on them to share his thoughts with others. Another method is a forum. This will allow him to take part in online discussions with others by writing posts that others can respond to.

24. Online communities: implications

Implementing an online community by setting up a forum could help the business understand customer needs. The forum would allow customers to post their comments directly to the business – the business can then respond to address customers' needs and concerns. A negative implication of the forum could be the implementation. A forum will take time to implement and run. There will also be costs involved, not just to set up but also to maintain, as the business will need to fix any problems and moderate comments.

25. Threats to data, information and systems

Malware are malicious software programs that infect computers and damage them by, for example, deleting or altering files or by stealing data. Examples of malware include viruses, trojans, worms and spyware. Being attacked by malware would potentially have a massive impact on Henley Investments as it could delete all the data they hold on customers who are investing with them, including their finances. This would likely cause the company to lose a massive amount of business due to the loss in reputation. Another threat to Henley Investments is accidental damage. This occurs due to human error, such as an employee accidentally deleting an important file, or a whole directory. While the impact may be less than with malware, it could still be significant and could cost them the business of any customers affected. It would certainly cause a loss in productivity until the data is recovered.

26. Protecting data: tools and techniques

Encryption is the process of converting data into an unreadable code known as ciphertext. This means that if someone steals the data it will still be safe as they will not be able to read the data while it is encrypted. However, if the encryption key is lost, Highcastle Advertising will not be able to access the data either. Anti-virus software is used to detect and remove malware from a computer system. It can also prevent viruses from infecting a computer system in the first place. Anti-virus software does need to be maintained though by regularly updating it, if Highcastle Advertising fail to do this their systems may no longer be secure.

27. Protecting data: legislation and codes of practice

The Data Protection Act is used to protect the privacy of people's personal data while it is being processed by anyone. If those processing an individual's data do not keep it private they can be fined hundreds of thousands of pounds. The Computer Misuse Act protects against attacks on computer systems where malicious users try to gain unauthorised access or spread viruses. If found guilty they can be punished by large fines and up to ten years in prison.

28. Features of online services

An example of an online service is a retail service. These include e-commerce websites and online auction websites. We use these in order to purchase items or services over the internet. This provides us with 24/7 access to shopping and saves on travelling costs. However, we may be bombarded by advertising emails and/ or texts after making online purchases. Another online service is news and information services such as traffic reports, weather reports and news websites. We use these to access the latest up-to-date information on a variety of topics. This can help us to plan for future travelling and events, such as checking out the traffic on our commute to work. We need to be sure the service we use provides the most up-to-date information possible, as changes in traffic situations happen very quickly. These can often be supplemented by the use of location aware services, providing content tailored to your location such as restaurant suggestions.

29. Business uses of online services

Meera could use online services to provide her target audience with incentives to use her; she could use social media platforms to target those who have special occasions coming up, making her business appear "at just the right time". Another alternative would be to use a website to sell her products online to new and existing customers. Allowing customers to see representations of her products would entice new sales. I think overall she could use a website to get people interested and use some targeted advertising to drive new customers to her website.

30. Uses and implications of IT systems

There are many ways that Lisa could use IT systems to help her keep track of things and promote her business. She could use some form of stock control, so that she knows exactly what stock she has of raw ingredients and keep track of what each cake costs more precisely. With this, she will then be able to identify where her costs are going and potentially find ways of reducing spending. She could also use IT to help promote her company. By using online advertising and social media, she could reach out to new customers, help her business to grow and increase her turnover.

31. Impact of IT systems on organisations

Ayisha could use online services for stock control. This could allow her supermarkets to automatically reorder stock, although it can be expensive and require training. The advantage of this for Ayisha is that stock shortages could be reduced, and she could make use of just in time ordering and supplier discounts due to ordering electronically. She could also use it for data logging, for example to record sales data, which she could then use for analysing the business performance and employee performance. However, she would need to be careful about using the data for staff appraisals without some safeguards in place.

32. Gathering data

One primary source of data is obtained using a questionnaire. This will allow Haldtech Ltd to gain feedback from a large audience in a small space of time. However, the questions are normally closed-ended, leading to a lack of depth in the answers, which Haldtech Ltd may need. Another primary source of data is interviews. This method will allow the company to ask follow-up questions to any answers in order to gain a greater depth of understanding, but it takes a long time to carry out and so they will only be able to hold interviews with a limited number of people.

33. Processing data

One validation method that could be used is a type check, which is used to ensure that the correct kind of data is entered, for example to make sure that only a date is entered into a date of birth field. Another validation method is a length check, for example on the password field to ensure the user chooses a password that is neither too short nor too long.
A verification method that could be used is a double entry check. This could be used on the password field, requiring the user to enter their password twice and checking that the two passwords match in order to ensure the user hasn't made an error.

34. Data presentation and trend analysis

Frank will already keep records of his sales and profits and he could use this data going back over a number of years to try and predict when he is likely to be busier. This is called trend analysis, and the more data he has, the more detailed this analysis should be and the more reliable any predictions are likely to be. He could identify, for example, that his café sales always increased from mid-November – then he could look at recruiting new staff before he gets too busy, thus giving himself time to train them properly. Combining the data over a number of years allows Frank to identify common patterns. Presenting the data as a chart of some kind makes it easy to notice these kinds of patterns.

35. Presenting data and results

One characteristic that a user interface must have is error reduction. This means that the interface must have methods in place for spotting and reporting errors in the data input, or to prevent the errors being made in the first place. For example, by implementing validation error messages, or providing controls such as spinners or drop down boxes to select from pre-defined lists. Another characteristic is intuitiveness. It should be clear to the user how to make use of the interface and how to enter data and navigate it. This can be done using good labelling and the use of features, such as pop up instructions to guide users, for example.

36. Moral and ethical issues 1

Online behaviour is a moral and ethical issue. It is the responsibility of users communicating their views online to behave acceptably and not to become insulting or abusive. This is commonly known as netiquette. Cyberbullying and trolling are common ethical problems associated with poor online behaviour. Another ethical issue is freedom of speech, which is our right to express views. Some see the closing of groups and accounts on social media pages as an infringement of the right to freedom of speech.

37. Moral and ethical issues 2

Computer misuse is an ethical issue that affects businesses gathering personal information. The online business must ensure it has measures in place to prevent misuse of personal information being stored. Privacy is another ethical issue here. People have a right to their privacy and so the business must only gather and store the information that they need.

38. Legislation protecting users and data

Simon is breaking the Copyright, Designs and Patents Act (1998) which protects the rights of the people who create original work such as music. Simon could face up to ten years in prison and an unlimited fine for sharing the music.

39. Legislation ensuring accessibility

The Equality Act is the main piece of legislation for protecting people with disabilities from being unfairly treated based on their disability. This act aims to ensure that employers and service providers will put in place reasonable facilities to ensure that disabled people can make use of their IT systems. The BSI codes of practice are guidelines that, among other things, help ensure that websites are accessible to people with disabilities. The Web Content Accessibility Guidelines also define good practice for making sure websites are accessible. This will help ensure people with disabilities will be able to access a business's website fairly.

40. Your Unit 1 exam

User experience (are the users experienced with the choices of hardware, software and operating systems?)
User needs (do any users require assistive technologies to enable them to access the computer systems? The organisation will need to consider any individual needs.)

41. Using case studies

Protection of data is an important consideration for Olivia. With cloud storage the data is available externally over the internet and so under threat from hackers who could gain access to the cloud storage and steal the data. They could use the data for identity theft, for example.

Privacy might also be an issue, as cloud storage is often used to share files and folders between multiple users. Olivia must ensure only the people who need to see the data can do so, so that the data is not misused, such as for blackmail purposes.

42. Long answer questions

In an exam, your response plan may be structured as below, with each bullet being presented as a detailed part of a larger report. However, other answers will be possible if they cover similar points.
You should provide an evaluation of the business's decision, stating if you think the decision is appropriate or not. Your evaluation should be supported by relevant points which may include:

- Employee experience – do the employees have experience with using the social networking and blogs in order to make use of maintaining these systems? If not then heavy training may be required which increases costs to the business for implementing the system.
- Customer needs – customers may not want these channels in order to communicate with staff and might prefer easier phone contact, etc. Therefore this would be a misuse of time, staff and money.
- Cost – implementing and running social media channels could be expensive for the business and require specialist staff. Are the potential benefits greater than the drawbacks to the business?
- Implementation – when does the system need to be implemented by and is this a reasonable expectation for the business, given any training requirements?
- Replacement/integration with current systems – review what current systems are in place. Comment on whether this is replacing a current system within the business or whether it needs to integrate with current systems?
- Productivity – the increased time spent in maintaining the social media channels could distract staff from other tasks and reduce productivity within the business. However, it could reduce staff time on phone calls, etc. when communicating with customers.
- Working practices – will any staff require a change in their normal job description to maintain this system? Will they need additional support, training or time in order to complete this work?

- Security – what data will be shared on the social media channels being used? Could it potentially put the customer personal information at risk?

43. Short answer questions

Mouse
Keyboard
Graphics tablet

44. 'Draw' questions

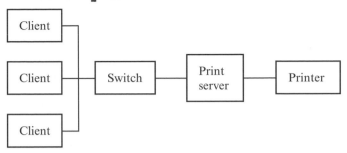

45. 'Explain' questions

JPG would be an appropriate format for Louise as it uses lossy compression that can reduce the size of the file to make it easier to send over email.
PNG is another format that could be useful. It uses lossless compression to reduce the file size. This won't reduce as much as JPG but the quality can be restored to its uncompressed state later.

46. 'Analyse' questions

In an exam, your response may look like the following, but other answers will be possible if they cover similar points.
You should provide an analysis of the decision, stating if the decision is appropriate or not. Your analysis should be supported by relevant points which may include:

- Disk defragmenter – this reorganises the data on Donna's hard disk so that data is no longer fragmented. This reduces file access times so she can load data from disk faster. This won't help if Donna is using an SSD though or if her disk is not very fragmented.
- Anti virus – the poor performance of Donna's computer may be due to malware on the system such as viruses or spyware. Anti-virus software will detect viruses on her system and remove them. It will also help prevent new viruses from being contracted. It must be kept up to date for it to detect the latest malware.
- Registry cleaners – old redundant registry entries exist on most systems as users add and delete software. This can reduce performance of the system. Registry cleaners can detect these redundant registry entries and remove them.
- System monitors – this monitors how resources like CPU and memory are being used to identify where problems are being caused so this can be addressed. It doesn't improve performance on its own though and requires good technical knowledge to make use of it.
- Any other relevant answers.

47. 'Evaluate' questions

In an exam, your response may be structured as below, but other answers will be possible if they cover similar points.
You should provide an evaluation of the types of data, stating if you think the data is appropriate for your research or not. Your evaluation should be supported by relevant points which may include:

Primary sources

- Questionnaire – this method will allow the student to gather information with specific questions from a large audience. This can be done anonymously which can improve honesty in answers. Response times can be low so this means wasted resources. Also, this method doesn't allow for much depth of understanding as follow-up questions can't be asked.

- Focus groups – this method will allow the student to gather information from a large group of people and use interaction between participants to gain more understanding and detailed answers. This method will take a long time for the student to organise and the data can be harder to analyse as it is less quantitative than questionnaires.
- Interviews – this method will allow the student to ask follow-up questions to get precise answers and detailed understanding of each respondent's thoughts. It takes a lot of time to carry out interviews and the data is harder to analyse as it is not quantitative.

Secondary sources

- Books – the data is normally very authoritative as books are normally written by experts and the facts will have been checked. However, it may take a long time for the student to find the information they want and the exact information may not be available. Data is likely to be less timely than that gained from primary sources.
- Websites – these are very cheap for the student to access and it is very easy to search for what they want. There is also a huge range of sources. However, the validity and reliability of data is difficult to judge as anyone can create a website, not just experts. It can also be difficult to judge whether the data is up to date.
- Magazines – these are good for timely data as magazines are dated and regularly released. It can be difficult to find the exact information needed though and can be expensive as the student might have to purchase a wide range of magazines to get the required information.

Unit 2: Creating Systems to Manage Information

48. Relational database management systems (RDBMS)

Term		Definition	
1	Primary key	d	A unique identifier
2	Tuple (or record)	a	A table row
3	Relation	b	Another name for a table
4	Attribute (or field)	c	A table column
5	Domain	f	The range of acceptable values
6	Cardinality	e	The number of records in a table

49. What are entities?

1 Entities: Student, Class, Tutor, Course.
2 Relationships:
   - Students belong to a class.
   - Tutors are responsible for students/students are allocated to tutors.
   - Students study on a course.

50. Entity relationships: one-to-one and one-to-many

A player belongs to or plays for a team. One team has many players so it's a one-to-many relationship. Usually a player can only play for one team.

51. Entity relationships: many-to-many

This is usually resolved by having an Order Lines table which has one record for each product that appears on an order.

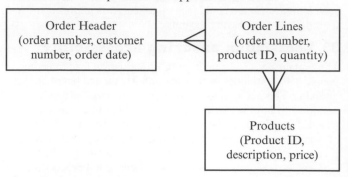

52. Relational keys

Customers place orders (one-to-many relationship). Primary key for the Customer table would be customer ID. Primary key for the Orders table would be order number. The customer ID is placed in the Order table as a foreign key so we can tell which customer placed each order.

The Orders table would need to be split into Order Header and Order Lines. The primary key from the Order Header table (order number) would be placed in the Order Lines table so users know which order the lines belong to. The Order Lines table could use a composite key made up of order number and line number.

The Products table would have a primary key of Product ID. This would be used as a foreign key in the Order Lines table so we know the details of the products ordered.

The Suppliers table would have a primary key of Supplier ID. This would be placed in the Products table as a primary key so we know which supplier supplies the product.

53. Database integrity

Referential integrity involves ensuring that there are no anomalies between related tables. For example, there should be no foreign key values in a table for which there are no corresponding records on the related table. If this does occur it can create 'lost' records, such as orders for which there are no customers.

Physical integrity is about protecting the data stored in the database from damage or loss, such as through hardware failure. Referential and physical integrity are important because databases often contain vital information which businesses and other organisations rely on for their day-to-day operations. So the loss of the data can have serious consequences.

54. Relational algebra

1	Join	c	combines two tables which have at least one common field.
2	Select	d	selects records from a table based on a given criterion.
3	Intersect	b	combines two tables, selecting just the records which occur in both.
4	Union	a	combines two tables which have the same fields.

55. Normalisation

1 Manufacturer, Price, Processor type and speed, Other hardware details.
2 There are two other repeating groups. Genre is one of them but there is not much more information about this data that could be added so it is not really worth moving to another table. Publisher is also a repeating group and would be a better choice to move to another table because there is more data that could be added about this table.

56. The stages of normalisation

a 2NF c 3NF
b 1NF d 1NF

57. Data dictionary

Example answer:

Table name	Console
Field name	**Attributes**
Console_ID	Primary Key, integer
Console_name	Text, 25 characters, no validation
Console_manufacturer	Text, 25 characters, no validation
Price	Currency data type, must be more than £50 and less than £500
Disk_Size_GB	Integer
Case_colour	Text, 10 characters, uses a lookup table with values 'Black', 'White' and 'Silver'

58. Manipulating data structures and data: SQL – Create and Insert

To add each record, use the SQL command Insert Into, for example:

```
INSERT INTO Cars
VALUES(1, 'VW', 'Golf', 5, 1600, 46,
115);
```

59. Manipulating data structures and data: SQL Select

(a) `SELECT Model, Engine_size FROM Cars WHERE Make = "Ford";`

(b) `SELECT Make, Model FROM Cars WHERE No_of_doors = 4;`

(c) `SELECT * FROM Cars WHERE MPG > 40;`

60. Relational database design steps

a and b:

1 Understand user requirements – this involves understanding what the system needs to do and what entities are involved.

2 Create ERDs – this means developing relationship diagrams which show how the entities in the system are related.

3 Normalisation – this is the process of refining the data into separate related tables. The process is used to confirm the ERD models are correct.

4 Create data dictionary – this lists all the fields in each table, and specifies the data type for each field and any validation to be applied to the field.

5 Application design – create designs for the user interface of the system, including data input screens and menus.

6 Design queries and reports – this involves sketching the layout for each query and report, and specifying the fields to be displayed and criteria for the queries.

7 Create test plans – this means stating the tests you will carry out for data testing, as well as forms and the user interface, queries and reports.

61. Relational database design considerations

Physical modelling – the hardware required to implement the database system, including disk space requirements.

Prototype – a partially implemented version of a system used to demonstrate how the final version will look and operate.

Data protection – protection applied to personal information stored on databases, legally required by the Data Protection Act 1998.

Data conversion – techniques used to transfer data from an old system to a new one.

62. Design documentation: user interface design

Forename	First_name
Surname	Surname
DOB	Date_of_birth
Course	Course
Address	Home_address
Town	Town
Post code	Postcode
Phone number	Phone_number

[Cancel] [Save]

Database fields and the validation applied:

First_name text, no validation
Surname text, no validation
Date_of_birth date, must be in the past
Course text, must exist on the course table
Address text, no validation
Town text, no validation
Postcode text, may use an input mask to ensure the correct format
Phone-number text, may use an input mask to ensure the correct format

Note: The primary key value (ID_number) should use an AutoNumber data type which Access will add for you, so it should not be included in the form.

63. Design documentation: reports and task automation

Your Ticket		Admit One
Date: DD/MM/YY		Start time: HH:MM
Venue: Xxxxxxxxxxxxx		
Band performing:		Xxxxxxxxxxxxxxxxxxxx
Ticket serial number.		NNNNNNNNN

64. Design documentation: query design

Table	Students	Students	Students	Class
Field	ID_Number	First_name	Surname	Class_tutor
Criteria				[enter tutor name]
Sort	Ascending			

65. Design documentation: test plans

Data dictionary:

Table name	Course_units
Field name	**Attributes**
Unit_number	Primary Key, integer
Unit_name	Text, 25 characters, no validation
GLH	Integer, can only be 60, 90 or 120
Type_of_assessment	Text, 8 characters can only be Internal or External
Type_of_unit	Text, 9 characters can only be Mandatory or Optional

Test plan:

Test No.	Table/field	Input data	Expected outcome	Actual outcome
1	Unit_name	Software development	Accepted	
2	GLH	59	Rejected	
3	GLH	121	Rejected	
4	GLH	Five	Rejected	
5	GLH	90	Accepted	
6	GLH	60	Accepted	
7	GLH	120	Accepted	
8	Type_of_assessment	Optional	Rejected	
9	Type_of_assessment	Internal	Accepted	
10	Type_of_assessment	External	Accepted	
11	Type_of_unit	Internal	Rejected	
12	Type_of_unit	Mandatory	Accepted	
13	Type_of_unit	Optional	Accepted	

66. Creating, setting up and maintaining data tables

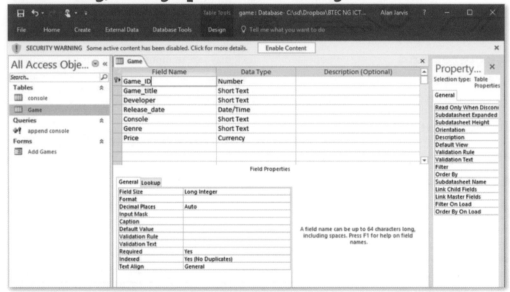

67. Data validation rules: lookup lists

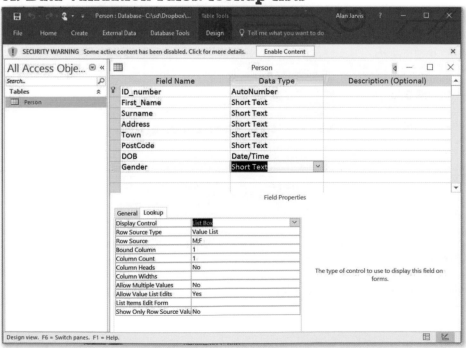

68. Data validation rules: comparison and Boolean operators

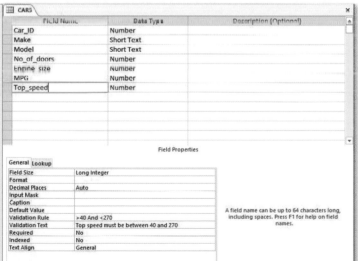

69. Validation rules: input masks

000"/"0000"/">A

70. Creating relationships

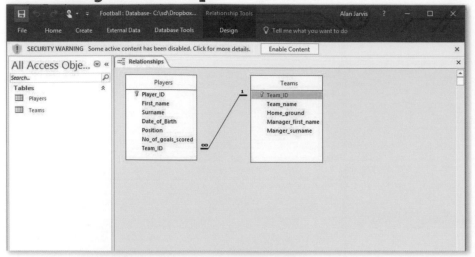

71. Generating output with queries

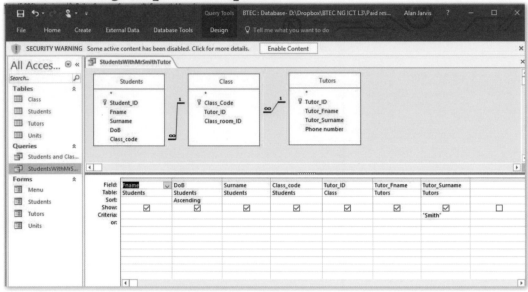

72. Queries using comparisons and multiple criteria

(a) Putting both criteria in the same row of the query grid would select those cars which had both an engine size of less than 1600 cc AND a top speed of over 110 mph.

(b) Putting one of the criteria in the 'or:' row would select all cars with either an engine size of less than 1600 cc OR a top speed of over 110 mph (so there would be more cars in this list).

73. Action queries

Action queries can select data from a table like normal queries, but the selected data can be inserted into a different table and fields.

74. User interface: creating and adjusting forms

75. User interface: adding automated features to form

76. User interface: applying security measures

1 A form not linked to any table.
2 In a table.
3 Autoexec.

77. Testing and refining the database solution

1 You can test:
   - tables and their validation rules
   - functionality of forms, queries and reports
   - referential integrity
   - security options.
2 You need to complete the test plan.
3 You need to record how you dealt with any errors you found and ensure you retest to ensure fixes work as expected.
4 The purpose of testing is to ensure a high-quality product which meets the user's requirements.

78. Evaluating the design process

My evaluation – the design stage

My first step in the design process was to go through the printout of the raw data and highlight the repeating groups of data. This gave me a good idea of what the separate tables will be. Next I tried to complete the normalisation process and got the data normalised to 1st and 2nd normal form, but I really couldn't work out what to do at the 3rd form stage. I decided to approach the problem in a different way and read the database scenario again carefully using a highlighter pen to identify the significant parts. Based on this, I sketched out an ERD diagram and I went through the normalisation steps again to see if the results confirmed what I had in the ERD. They did, so I was happy with the design of the tables and the relationships between them. I drew a final version of the ERD and started creating the data dictionary.

What I learned from this is that it is important to understand the scenario well as this really helps to understand how the data should be split into tables and the normalisation should be done in conjunction with a draft ERD rather than on its own.

79. Evaluating the development and testing process

Answers will vary, but could include:
- How well did my design match the final product?
- What went well during the development and what problems did I have?
- How did I overcome the problems?
- How clear and easy to use is the user interface?
- How effective was the testing at uncovering issues? Have I tested my database enough?
- If I had more time, how could I improve the database?
- If I developed the database again, what would I do differently?

80. About your set task

There is no one correct answer for this question – answers will vary.

81. The set task brief

1 Design the database structure, including normalising the data and drawing an ERD.
2 Create a data dictionary for the tables defined in the ERD, including any validation.
3 Create a test plan.
4 Create the tables and relationships in Access.
5 Create the menus and data input forms.
6 Create the queries.
7 Create the reports.
8 Test your database.
9 Review and evaluate.

82. The data

There is no written answer for this question – it is a chance for you to practise importing csv files into Access.

83. Activity 1: entity relationship diagram (normalisation)

1

Weigh-in_ID	Member_ID	Week	Weigh
1	1	1	95
2	1	2	90
3	1	3	90

Primary key   Foreign key

2 The link is made by inserting the primary key of the Member table (Member_ID) into the Weigh-in table as a foreign key.

84. Activity 1: entity relationship diagram (drawing the ERD)

1 It is a one-to-many relationship, with one member having many weigh-ins.

2

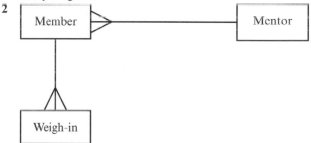

85. Activity 2: data dictionary

Table Name:	Mentor
Field name	**Attributes**
Mentor_ID	Primary key, 'autonumber' field generated by the software
F_name	Text data type, 25 characters, no validation
Surname	Text data type, 25 characters, no validation
Gender	Text data type, 1 character, must be M or F

Table Name:	Weigh-in
Field name	**Attributes**
Weigh-in_ID	Primary key, 'autonumber' field generated by the software
Member_ID	Integer data type, must exist on the Member table
Week	Integer data type, must be between 1 and 52
Weight	Integer data type, must be between 50 and 120

86. Activity 3: design specification – the user interface (forms)

Example designs:

a

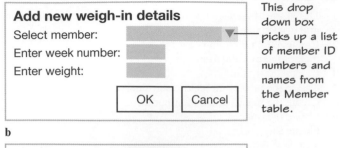

This drop down box picks up a list of member ID numbers and names from the Member table.

b

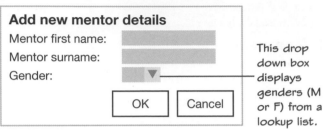

This drop down box displays genders (M or F) from a lookup list.

87. Activity 3: design specification – the user interface (queries)

Query design to output all the members allocated to a specific mentor:

Table	Member	Member	Member	Mentor	Mentor	Mentor	
Field	Member_ID	F_name	Surname	Mentor_ID	F_name	Surname	
Criteria					[Enter mentor First Name]	[Enter mentor surname]	
Sort							

88. Activity 3: design specification – the user interface (reports)

Query design:

Table	Member	Member	Member	Weigh-in	Weigh-in	
Field	F_name	Surname	Target_weight_kg	Week	Weight_kg	Difference_kg: [Weight_kg]–[Target_weight_kg]
Criteria	[Enter member First Name]	[Enter member surname]				
Sort						

Report design:

Member's Weight Loss Report

Member name: Xxxxxxxxx Xxxxxxxxx
Target weight nnnn kg

Week	Current weight	Weight to be lost
nn	nnnn kg	nnnn kg
nn	nnnn kg	nnnn kg
nn	nnnn kg	nnnn kg

89. Activity 4: testing plan

Examples of tests you could use:

Test No.	Purpose of test	Test data	Expected result	Actual result	Comment/actions
	Tests for the Mentor table				
1	F_name	Amy	Accepted		
2	Surname	Smith	Accepted		
3	Gender	Z	Rejected		
4	Gender	F	Accepted		
5	Gender	M	Accepted		
	Tests for the Weigh-ins table				
1	Member_ID (referential integrity)	99	Rejected		(No matching records on the Member table)
2	Member_ID (referential integrity)	1	Accepted		
3	Week	53	Rejected		
4	Week	Five	Rejected		
5	Week	5	Accepted		

90. Activity 5: database development

Examples of possible responses:

Add new weigh-in form:

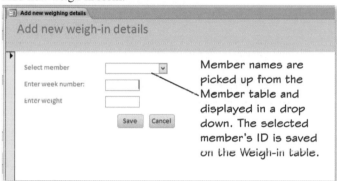

Member names are picked up from the Member table and displayed in a drop down. The selected member's ID is saved on the Weigh-in table.

Add new mentor form:

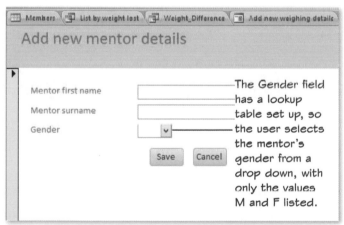

The Gender field has a lookup table set up, so the user selects the mentor's gender from a drop down, with only the values M and F listed.

Query design view to show all the members allocated to a specified mentor:

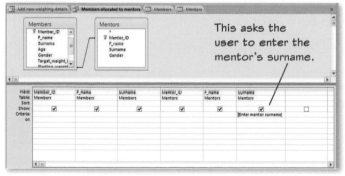

This asks the user to enter the mentor's surname.

The query result with Smith entered:

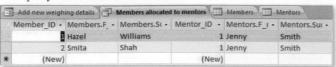

Query design view to show list of all the weigh-ins for a specified week, ranked by weight lost (compared to starting weight):

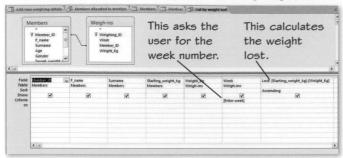

The query result with week number 2 entered:

Member_ID	F_name	Surname	Starting_we	Weight_Kg	Week	Lost
3	Clive	Hanson	90	85	2	5
1	Hazel	Williams	97	90	2	7
2	Smita	Shah	108	100	2	8
* (New)						

The completed report:

Weekly Weight Lost Report

Week	2			
Member name		Starting weight	Current weight	Weight lost
Smita	Shah	108	100	8
Hazel	Williams	97	90	7
Clive	Hanson	90	85	5

Query design view to show list of a specified member's weigh-ins, with the difference between each week's weight and their target weight shown:

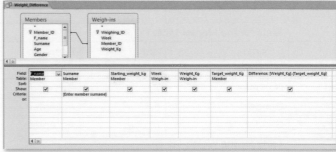

Query result with member surname 'Williams' entered:

F_name	Surname	Starting_we	Week	Weight_Kg	Target_weig	Difference
Hazel	Williams	97	1	95	75	20
Hazel	Williams	97	2	90	75	15
Hazel	Williams	97	3	90	75	15
*						

Completed report:

Member's Weight Loss Report

Member Name:	Hazel	Williams	Target_weight_Kg	75
Week	Current Weight		Weight to be lost	
1	95		20	
2	90		15	
3	90		15	

91. Activity 6: evaluation of your database solution

Check your answer against the lists on pages 78–79 . Did you include all the elements in your evaluation?

Notes

Notes

Notes